MAYBE YOU *WILL* SURVIVE

Statement of Purpose

The Holocaust spread across the face of Europe just a few decades ago. The brutality then unleashed is still nearly beyond comprehension. Millions of innocents—men, women and children—were consumed by its flames.

The goal of Holocaust Publications, a non-profit organization founded by survivors, is to publish and disseminate works on the Holocaust. These will include survivors' accounts, testimonies and memoirs, historical and regional analyses, anthologies, archival and source documents and other relevant materials that will help shed light on this cataclysmic era.

These books and studies will be made available to the general public, scholars, researchers, historians, teachers and students. They will be used in Holocaust Resource Centers, libraries and schools, synagogues and churches. They will help foster an increased awareness of the Holocaust and its implications. They will help to preserve the memory for posterity and to enable this awesome time to be better understood and comprehended.

Holocaust Library
216 West 18th Street
New York, NY 10011
212-463-7988

MAYBE YOU *WILL* SURVIVE

A True Story

by
Aron Goldfarb

HOLOCAUST LIBRARY
NEW YORK

Library of Congress Cataloging-in-Publication Data

Goldfarb, Aron, 1923-
    Maybe you will survive: the true story of Aron Goldfarb.
        p.   cm.
    ISBN 0-89604-153-0 (cloth): $24.95. — ISBN 0-89604-154-9 (pbk.):
    $12.95
    1. Jews — Poland — Białobrzegi (Radom) — Persecutions. 2. Holo-
caust, Jewish (1939-1945) — Poland — Białobrzegi (Radom) — Per-
sonal narratives. 3. Goldfarb, Aron, 1923-   . 4. Białobrzegi
(Radom, Poland) — Ethnic relations.
DS135.P62B5364   1991   91-2922
940.53′18′094384 — dc20   CIP

Cover Design by The Appelbaum Company

Printed in the United States of America

Dedicated in loving memory to my dear mother Sarah, my father Moishe and to my two courageous brothers Itzhak and Shimon, my beautiful sisters Esther and Brucha, all slain by the ravagers of another six million of our innocent people.

Preface

On September 1, 1939, after a number of fabricated border incidents, the armies of the Third Reich invaded Poland. Forty infantry divisions together with fourteen mechanized divisions crossed the open frontier with lightning speed and efficiency. The armies commanded by General Fedor von Bock struck northern Poland at Danzig and the Polish Corridor. At the same time, the stronger and larger army group under General Gerd von Rundstedt invaded central and southern Poland from Silesia, as well as the Slovakian and Moravian borders. Polish forces were numerically strong, but no match for the Luftwaffe, and the lightning speed of the German advance. By the eighth of September units of Germany's Tenth Army had thrust to the outskirts of Warsaw. Poland's forces were surrounded west of the rivers Vistula and Bug. All defenses were crushed.

On September 17, 1939, two Soviet army groups entered Poland from north and south of the Pripet

Marshes. Thus, whatever last lingering hopes remained of stemming the Nazi invasion were destroyed forever.

The very next day the Polish Government and high command crossed the frontier into Romania, and then into exile in London. On the twenty fourth of September, over one thousand Luftwaffe aircraft launched massive air raids against the city. The Warsaw garrison held out until September 28, followed two days later by a ground assault.

The nation, partitioned between Germany and the U.S.S.R., under the agreement of the secret Hitler-Stalin pact, had been brutalized and conquered. Its course of history had been unalterably changed.

This story is true. It is not a tale of tactics or strategy. Nor of heroes in battle. It is a saga of survival. Of one man's struggle and that of his family. However, as with all wars, there are no happy endings.

Part One

Chapter One

It was the middle of the night. He didn't know what time it was, only that it was during the silent hours before dawn. As he lay with the blanket pulled up to his neck, Aron could hear the distant howling of the wind whipping down from the hills, between the branches of the trees and along the cobblestones and dirt of Bialobrzegi's ancient winding streets. The shuttered windows were tightly closed and locked. Silver beams of bright moonlight filtered through the wooden slats, forming interesting patterns across the beamed ceiling of the single room cottage. Aron was aware that he was drifting somewhere between sleep and wakefulness. A hazy semi-consciousness.

Things were no longer the same, he thought to himself. And they never would be. His youthful years of innocence were left behind. Shattered almost overnight by this new and grim reality of fear that permeated everyone around him.

By most European standards, Aron would still be considered a child. One of the rabbi's five sons. A thin curly-headed fifteen year old who should have been setting his mind on his future, chasing pretty girls like Rachel Weisbord, and falling in love for the first time.

Love? The very word had lost all meaning for him. There was no such thing as love anymore, nor was there any future to contemplate. Not for him—not for anyone. Only the fear remained, etched indelibly into his consciousness. Daunting fear. A sadistic apprehension that kept one's heart pounding and palms wet. Purposeful, the way the invaders wanted it to be. Keeping them all in a state of constant nerve-wracking anxiety.

Who would live and who would die tomorrow. When would they all be taken away? These were the unspoken topics in his once peaceful town of Bialobrzegi. Its disheartened, simple people huddled in obscurity along the desolate streets, conversing in whispers before the dreaded eight p.m. curfew, terrified of being overheard by suspicious neighbors, strangers, or the ever-vigilant soldiers that prowled relentlessly.

Worst of all, Aron realized, was the terrible paranoia that had gripped and swept across Poland like a biblical plague. His Poland; his home, his country.

Not long before, the streets of the town had been crowded with people. So many sounds everywhere. Laughter, gaiety, the active markets crammed with shoppers during the day, the strolling of lovers in the evening and the town's many visitors. The constant groaning of old wooden wagons with creaking wheels making their way south and north along the bustling Warsaw-Radom road, bringing goods to and from the capital.

4

Those had been good times for Aron, times of boisterous dares by young men taunting each other in fun. The giggles of girls being teased by the local boys. There were the shouts of children playing soccer on the grass. Jews versus gentiles, competing as friendly rivals, not as enemies.

Now all that had disappeared. What had changed it? He didn't understand the reasons. Not even Papa could explain it to him. Weren't the Germans the cultured descendants of Goethe and Schiller? A people known for the creation of great literature, music, science, renowned for its sophistication?

There would be no more soccer matches in Bialobrzegi. All its past was now buried deeply in time and memories, never to return, Aron knew. It was replaced instead with the ominous thuds of boots. Nazi, fascist ones, harsh against the gray cobblestone. The fearful shouts at night of halt as some soldier caught a hapless soul darting across the shadowy alleys. And then, perhaps most fearful of all, the distant sounds of gunfire.

Bialobrzegi had been a beautiful little town, nestled at the edge of a forest beside the winding and scenic River Pileca, about eighty kilometers south of Warsaw. A resort town, a place very much out of a storybook, where visitors from the big city might come to stay for a few days or a week to enjoy the air, the serenity, and the bracing cool waters. A brand new bridge of gleaming steel and concrete spanning magnificently across the shimmering river as you entered the town. After school, Aron and his friends would run to the river's banks to lie in the deep grass and watch in wonder, as the lumbering heavy machinery went into motion, gasping as the bridge slowly took graceful shape and fanned far across both banks.

5

Maybe I'll become an engineer and build bridges like this, Aron thought. *Or perhaps I'll study architecture at the University.*

After all, wasn't anything possible for a young man who aggressively pursues what he wants? Papa always told him that a man who takes his studies seriously could possess the whole world. Isn't that also what Papa taught his pupils in the Hebrew and Bible classes he taught at home? And hadn't Mama believed this too before she died?

Aron shook his head in bewilderment. Those memories were so far removed from the present reality. University educated engineers were not needed for digging graves. Architects weren't necessary to set grave stones in the cemetery. Nazi Germany had removed the last vestiges of decency from the soul of Europe.

Whose turn to die might it be tonight? Some star-crossed lover slipping from a sweetheart's arms? A boy found foraging in the fields of nearby farms for something to eat? A poor lost soul who lost his way and was caught after curfew? There was no way of knowing, nor did it really matter to the occupiers.

The military police might have caught him and brought him in for questioning, perhaps tortured him, maybe condemned him to the hell of a labor camp. If the prisoner was lucky, Aron believed, his captors would kill him instantly and leave his bloodied corpse in some street or alley as a warning to other transgressors. At least his pitiful suffering would have ended. Then the old men at the synagogue could chant the Hebrew prayer for the dead.

Bialobrzegi had been sealed off from the outside world; closed by the Germans with their endless supply of trucks, guns, and vicious guard dogs. The townspeople barely eked out a living from day to day, fully aware of what was happening, but helpless to do anything about it.

To his right, Simon stirred in his sleep. He yawned. "Aron . . ."

Aron turned towards his little brother who lay curled up at the edge of the large bed. "Go back to sleep," he whispered sternly. "Or you'll wake the others."

There were two beds in the room. Aron shared his with his younger brother and his father. Across from them lay his older sister, Ester, together with her handsome husband, and Aron's sister, Brucha, only a year and a half younger than he. Aron loved his family deeply, and in many ways was more worried about them than he was for himself.

His older brothers, Yitzhak and Abe, no longer lived at home. They were taken away by the SS to work for them. The feared special police kept a close watch on all those they consigned to labor, so Yitzhak and Abe were not permitted to return home at night. Instead, they were bunked at SS headquarters in a nearby village called Sucha, situated in the middle of a vast mountainous forest. It was Aron's aim and hope to find and join them, then together run from this hell and hide in the scrub of the dense Polish forests. There, maybe, his brothers and he might elude their omnipotent enemy, and fight back. Attack the Germans? What with? A rag tag army against the might of the Wehrmacht?

Simon rubbed his eyes. They were wide, and very innocent.

"I had a dream, Aron," he muttered. "A strange dream."

Aron hushed him, patting the boy's head. "Tell me all about it tomorrow, alright?"

"But it was about Jacob."

7

The mention of his third older brother made Aron wince. Jacob had dared to take his chances and flee across the eastern frontier, escaping to Russia. Aron knew he would have done the same, but then, who would remain for Simon? He could not allow all the burden to fall on his father's weary shoulders. No, he realized that he was too closely tied to his family, to all of them. He would have to stay—at least for now—and help to take care of the family. Other opportunities would surely present themselves. He was constantly fantasizing about them. Someday, that was his vow, his promise to himself.

Someday.

"Jacob was being tortured." Simon continued. "In my dream, he was crying out to me—to all of us, to find him; to rescue him." The child looked at Aron pleadingly. "Is Jacob really safe?" he demanded to know. Simon adored his older brother, and if Aron told him that something was so, then it was.

"Of course he's safe." assured Aron.

"How do you know?"

"Because I know."

Simon wasn't satisfied. "Do you think the Russians will hurt him?"

Aron drew a deep breath and exhaled slowly. A dog barked nearby. "He's as safe as he can be," he answered. "Russia is no friend of the Nazis. They'll help him. They have to." Aron spoke with as much conviction as he could muster, but deep inside, he wasn't certain at all. How could the Russians be trusted? They had always been an enemy of Poland. Always the rabid foes of the Jews. Yet Jacob had believed and trusted them. He proved it by placing his life in their hands. Aron felt confused by it all. The only thing he could do was pray; pray that Jacob was really safe, and not exiled to some distant Soviet labor camp, or worse.

8

"Aron," Simon said after a moment, "why are you working for the Germans?"

"I have no choice, either, like Abe and Yitzhak."

"Do they beat you?"

He shook his head. "No. I'm a good worker. I don't create problems for them. They like me."

For the past several months he'd been working on the Zeork power line. Digging holes in the ground, mixing the cement, and packing it around the huge steel poles being lowered deep into the soft earth. The Germans were always aware of his every move. Their cold eyes were firmly fixed on the groups of unfortunate laborers, guard dogs always at their sides, unmoving.

A German builder, *Meister* Emil, was Aron's foreman on the huge project. The German military had entrusted him with the task of constructing the power line's foundations, which stretched on for untold kilometers. Aron knew that he had worked as hard as he could, and never tried to play any games. Because of his productive efforts *Meister* Emil had requested that Aron be assigned to him personally as one of his regular crew. About thirty sturdy young men had been selected for the job. Aron met all the necessary qualifications: he was strong, smart, and not a troublemaker. With his job came the important documents, all officially stamped and approved by the German occupying authorities.

He always kept his papers buttoned in the pocket of his shirt, even at night while he slept. It was that precious to him.

Once *Meister* Emil told him, "This is a very special document you've been given, Aron. Appreciate it. Should anything happen to the Jews of your town you'll be able to remain here and work with us." Left unspoken by *Meister* Emil was the fact that this validated paper would protect him from removal to the concentration camps. Others would have to go, but not him. A good worker always had another day's labor scheduled; yet one more tomorrow, another day of life. His work papers were a lifeline that many would unhesitatingly kill to obtain.

"Will I have to work for the Germans, too?" Simon wanted to know.

"No. You're too young."

"Then will they shoot me like the others?"

"Don't ever say that, Simon!" Anger showed in Aron's weary features. "Do you hear me?"

Tears welled in the boy's eyes.

Aron immediately regretted his outburst. "No," he added softly to Simon. "They won't shoot you. You'll be safe."

The reality of their existence, however, was far more precarious than his assurances indicated. German soldiers prowled the Jewish ghetto constantly; blustering through the narrow streets, bursting into homes at random and seizing the residents. How often he had heard the screams, the begging, then the burst of gunfire. Sometimes their victims were shot down in cold blood, on other occasions they were hanged from a makeshift gallows. The bodies were often left swaying from the branches of the trees, lifeless legs dangling, heads bowed and faces bloodless. Terror was apparent in their lifeless faces.

Nor could there be anything worse than the staring accusative eyes of the dead. . . .

Aron shuddered at the thought.

In the town there were also men like Koszla. He was a collaborator, moving around Bialobrzegi with the police, and singling out particular homes.

10

"Here lives a rich Jew," Koszla would tell them.

Then he would stand back in the shadows and watch sadistically while the house was broken into and the family dragged away. What sort of a man was this Koszla? What sort of human being would take pleasure in the suffering and deaths of others? Perhaps, though, men like him were not human at all.

Often, after such mindless slaughterings, the Germans would rouse other Jews or Poles in the town and force them to bury the dead. Koszla would usually oversee this work and attest for his masters that it was being done properly. He would also listen diligently for whispered treasonous talk. He would look for those who might openly condemn him or his German overlords. Then they, too, would become fodder for Koszla's grisly mill. If there was one thing that Aron wished, it was the chance to kill this despised informer before he fled into the forests. But then, another would take his place. Koszla's death might also mean the end of his entire family in retribution. Nothing was worth that price. Nevertheless, Aron was certain that that day would come. Oh yes, it surely would. For the time being he—and everyone else—could only bide their time.

Those who were more fortunate could have their whole family relocated in various work camps. The Germans needed laborers urgently. It was a small condolence, but at least there was a possibility of surviving this horror, that must sooner or later come to an end.

So for the present, they always slept in their clothes, realizing that merely not moving fast enough on command, was reason enough for the Germans to kill you on the spot. Each member of Aron's family had their

11

pitiful little bundle of belongings always ready, should they be roused in the middle of the night; an extra shirt, a pair of socks, a change of underwear.

"It'll be morning soon, Simon. Try to go back to sleep. Papa will wake up and be very angry."

To his left, the six-foot-one, red-bearded, blue-eyed, strapping man lay still and deep in his dreams. Aron turned towards the silhouette of his father. How could he ever put into words the pride and love he felt for him.

Sleep well, Papa. And don't worry. You're not alone. I'm here with you. . . .

Chapter Two

The evening was chilly, the sun had already set behind the horizon of hills and trees. In the twilight Aron walked wearily towards his home. Fallen autumn leaves covered the ground. It was October, the High Holy Days of *Rosh Ha'Shana* and *Yom Kippur* had barely passed.

A kerosene odor was pervasive as he came through the door of the cottage. Supper was waiting. Ester, an apron tied around her slender waist, looked over at the tired youth from beside the wooden stove. Lamplight outlined her full figure, giving her the look of a finely crafted sculpture. Next to her stood Brucha, herself a budding young woman, with long red hair reaching down to her shoulders. Brucha, as always, had been helping her sister with the cooking.

"Why are you so late?" Ester asked with knitted brows as she smoothed her apron. "I was beginning to worry about you."

Aron forced a weak smile and waved the question off. He was unwilling to discuss the day's events. Ester didn't press him as he sniffed the air like a hungry puppy. "Something smells good. Soup tonight?"

She nodded, smiling broadly. "We have potatoes, too. And fresh bread."

"Fresh bread?"

"Papa got it," volunteered Simon. The boy grinned up at his older brother. Aron lifted him and swung him around. "You've probably eaten half the loaf already, I'll bet."

"I did not!"

Aron laughed and set him down, throwing aimless punches while Simon ducked and threw a few harmless jabs of his own.

"Where's Papa?"

"Outside, washing, waiting for you to come." Ester frowned. She noticed that his clothes were more than a little dirty. "It might be a good idea if you washed your hands and face as well."

Aron agreed; he stepped outside and immediately saw the tall frame of his father. Moshe Goldfarb was a man of fifty, well built, strong, and in good health. But the lines around his tired eyes and his furrowed brow attested to the pain and suffering he had endured. He wore a skullcap, which covered his slightly balding pate. The red beard was long and still fiery.

"Hello, Papa."

Moshe removed the watch from his vest pocket. An engraved wedding gift that had withstood a generation of frequent use. The chain dangled as he snapped the cover open. "It's well after seven, Aron. You're later than usual. Was there any trouble for you today?"

"No, Papa, no trouble." Aron averted his father's piercing gaze. Papa had a way of looking right through

14

you. Knowing what you're thinking, and aware of everything, it seemed.

"Are you sure?" He put his beloved watch away. Looking at the time had become a habit, he did it constantly.

"I'm sure, Papa. I'm sure."

"Don't hide anything from me, son." Moshe scrutinized the boy. His clothes weren't torn, nor were there any evident signs of a scuffle. However, he knew his son's restless nature. He realized that the same hidden fires that years ago had stirred inside himself now did so in Aron. "Tell me if anything's wrong," he said softly to his son.

"I . . . I guess I was just doing some thinking, Papa. That's all. Just lost in thought."

"Thinking about what?" Moshe was not satisfied. "Running away again? Leaving home? Like Jacob did?"

"Jacob was forced to leave. He had no choice, remember? The Germans accused him of stealing."

Moshe was nobody's fool. His many years of experience as a religious teacher had taught him only too well to recognize when something was amiss. Everyday for years now he'd been giving orthodox religious instruction in afternoons to a number of the town's Jewish children. He conducted his classes in shifts, sometimes five, sometimes ten students at a time. His love of Judaism, its long history, culture, and its traditions had never left him. It was only enhanced as he grew older, as did his understanding of human nature. He knew instantly that something was troubling Aron.

"No, Papa, I'm not thinking of doing what Jacob did. It isn't like that at all."

"But you have been thinking of leaving again?"

Aron hung his head. There was no point in trying to

15

deny it. He had been taught never to lie to his father. "Yes, Papa, I have been thinking about it. I've never stopped thinking about it. But you already knew that."

With a long sigh, Moshe put his arm around the boy and held him close. "I will not stop you, you know that, son. I would *never* stop you, as I did not stand in Jacob's way. You, as all men, have a will of your own. You must do as your conscience dictates."

Aron looked at him intently. "Then I think we should all leave here, Papa. Run away, as fast as we can. All of us together, now." He blurted out his feelings with conviction.

"And go where?"

"Does it really matter? To the forests. They'd never find us there. Others have done it. We could stay in hiding for many years if necessary."

The rabbi shook his head slowly but firmly. "No, Aron. I cannot go, nor can your sisters. Neither Ester nor Brucha could survive such an ordeal. And someone has to remain behind to protect them. Just as someone must stay here and speak for the Jews of this town."

"Since when do German soldiers listen to what Jews have to say? I wish they were dead, all of them." Aron was angry. "I hope that one day England or Russia wipes Germany off the face of the earth."

Moshe looked down at him with a hint of sadness. "Hitler does not speak for all of his people. Germany has never before been our enemy—"

"Until now. Please open your eyes, Papa. We are all doomed if we remain here. One way or another, they will kill us. You know it, too. It's happening all around us, every day, and night. This afternoon I watched as they flogged a boy. They only laughed as he begged them to stop beating him. *Laughed,* Papa." Tears appeared in the corners of Aron's eyes, and he tried to hide them.

"I understand how you must feel, son."

"But they didn't stop; not until he lay sprawled in the dirt and could no longer move. There were bruises all over his bloody face. When we tried to pick him up they told us to leave him there . . ." He bit his quivering lip.

Moshe inhaled deeply and raised himself to his full height. "Now I understand what happened today."

"Please, Papa. Listen to me. Let's run away. Tonight. Before its too late. *Please.*"

"Wash your face and come inside, Aron. We don't want Ester to be angry with us."

Aron swallowed hard and said nothing. There was no point in arguing with Papa. His views were as firmly rooted as was his religion. His mind would not be changed.

Slowly, sadly, Aron went to the water pump. From the corner of his eye he saw his father enter the house. His shoulders were slightly stooped, his gait fraught with pain. Moshe Goldfarb, the man of the book, the man of wisdom, did not have an answer for his son.

"What are you doing, Aron?"

Simon sidled up to his brother as he sat relaxing under an elm tree. It was a cloudless night, and at the sound of his little brother's voice Aron stopped his star gazing. "What time is it?"

"Almost eight; curfew. Ester told me to get you inside right away. No excuses, she said."

"You go. I'll be along presently."

The same streak of stubbornness that was an integral part of Aron was also a trait of his younger brother.

17

Shaking his head in refusal, he said, "I'll go when you go. We still have a few minutes, I guess."

Simon's hair was the same fiery red as Papa's. Aron's was black. Only his and his mother's were different. "You never do as you're told, do you?"

"Do you?" Simon retorted boldly.

"No, I suppose not. Papa says I got that from Mama. I guess you did too."

Simon lay on his back, folding his arms against the autumn chill. It was getting colder every day. Soon October would pass into November, and the long hard Polish winter would begin.

"Do you remember much about Mama, Aron? What she was like, I mean?"

"Sure. Don't you?" He thought the better of it. Simon had been little more than a toddler. "No, you were still very young. Really just a baby. But isn't there anything you can recall?" It made him sad to think that his brother didn't really know anything about the woman who gave birth to all of them.

"Not very much, I don't think. Ester is always urging me to remember, reminding me of things we once did together, but I don't know." He grimaced and shrugged. "Please tell me what she was like."

"What Mama was like?"

The wind was picking up, rustling through the old trees, causing the heavy branches to sway. Dark clouds were gathering above the distant horizon, rolling swiftly. It would probably rain tomorrow.

Aron sat and thought long before he answered. "To me Mama was always very beautiful. I recall her long braided hair, falling along down her back. Always gleaming, especially in the sunlight. Sometimes she would wear a white blouse, as pristine as new snow,

18

and a long black skirt. Other times she would wear her shawl before she left for the market."

As Simon listened fascinated, a flood of memories came streaming back to Aron, and along with them a child's sorrow for a mother he knew he would never see again.

He always enjoyed being near Mama, all of the time, but especially when they went to the market together. To the then five-year old Aron being there reminded him of a grown-up's wonderland. The narrow aisles crowded with eager shoppers, the vendors hawking their wares and foodstuffs. Freshly slaughtered chickens hanging upside down in the endless stalls, great bins overflowing with fresh vegetables and produce brought in daily from the local farms along with eggs, fruit, cheeses, and goat's milk. Shoppers would examine all the wares, haggling, bartering, and comparing prices.

"Herrings," one merchant would cry out. "Twenty herrings for only one *slota*." This was quickly followed by a competitor, shouting, "I have twenty-one herrings for one *slota*!" Everything could be found within the fascinating world of Bialobrzegi's marketplace: from fine fabrics to imported butter, from earthenware to shoes, candy and chocolate, milk and vodka. It was the bakery, however, that Aron enjoyed the most. Whoever was shopping that day with Mama was sure to receive a freshly baked, steaming hot roll, so soft it would melt in your mouth. That extra roll, so small, so very little to ask for, had been something Aron knew he would never forget.

Thursdays and Fridays were Mama's cooking days, Thursday was designated exclusively for baking. He recalled Mama and his sisters going to the cupboard, taking out the flour, sugar, and butter. Very soon, the entire house would be filled with the appetizing aromas of hot baked pretzels, Mama's own delicious cookies, and *challah* bread. On Saturday, the Sabbath, her kitchen, of course, was closed. His home was a very orthodox one, and although meat was a rarity, not affordable during the week, Mama always put a little money aside for special Friday and Saturday dinners—usually a nice plump chicken.

Aron sat staring at the stars again, but in his mind's eye Mama was standing right there in front of him, alive, very real, leaning by the table during Sabbath supper, her slim hands covering her girlish face and eyes, intoning the Sabbath prayers as she would light the candles.

"Don't you even remember going to the synagogue on Friday nights, Simon? Papa would hold out his hands and everybody held onto one of his fingers?"

The child shook his head. Aron regarded his little brother sadly. It was such a shame that Simon had no recollections at all. A real misfortune. He was all the more elated that his own memories were so real, so fresh in his mind. He never wanted to forget them, and he knew that he never would.

"We were a very poor family, Simon," he said at last, "but still exceedingly rich in many ways."

"Papa tells us that all the time. To be grateful for what we have, and to count our blessings."

"Yes. And Papa is right." He squeezed Simon's hand. "As long as we have each other, and are honest with ourselves and our fellow men, we'll be all right. Jealousy of others only hurts us. I know that Mama believed that as well."

Simon hesitated before his next question. "How did she die, Aron?"

"Oh, she became sick, seriously ill. I was just about

your age now, when it happened. She had cancer, and three of the doctors in our town would regularly come to the house to treat her. They couldn't do much, they told Papa. Mama needed to be taken to a hospital. Then, one day her brother, our uncle Jacob, bundled her in blankets, wrapped a scarf around her head and put her in his cart. The horse pulled that cart all the way to the city, Simon. All the way to Warsaw to the Czeste Hospital. Mama had to see a special doctor on the staff there, someone who treated people with her illness. But it was very expensive. We didn't know how we could pay his fee. So Papa had to sell just about everything he owned to try to raise the money.

Simon started to cry as Aron talked. Aron too wept, but he kept turning away so Simon could not see him. He continued the story with a lump in his throat.

"It was sometime before Passover, around *Purim*, I think, when Uncle Jacob finally brought Mama home. There was snow on the ground. He carefully carried her into the house and placed her gently on her bed. Then she hugged us all, one at a time. God, I was so happy to see her back home again. However, I noticed that Papa was standing back in the shadows, away from the rest of us. He was trying his utmost not to cry, and not to look upset for our sakes and for Mama's. I don't know if anyone else saw him, although I think Brucha probably did. She seemed scared."

Poor Brucha, Aron thought. *Sometimes I think the situation has been more burdensome for her. She tries so hard to help Ester, and she's so young. . . .*

"Mama asked our brother Jacob to read to her from the *Magilla*," Aron continued. "The *Purim* story must have given her some comfort. He read it softly to her and she smiled.

"I stood close by, staring at her all the time. Her face

21

was brightened by the glow of the kerosene lamp. She didn't look well. She became so thin all of a sudden, so frail. Her skin was yellow, and she seemed to be very tired. Mama must have noticed me gazing intently at her because she called me to her. Suddenly there was a brightness in her eyes. 'Don't worry, Aron,' she told me. 'I'm going to be alright.' I wanted to believe her. I really tried. I nodded when she smiled up at me. I'll never forget that look on her face, Simon. She was so happy to see me, but she also seemed so sad.

He paused, sitting with his knees up, and his arms wrapped tightly around them, vividly recollecting those dark, discouraging days.

"Mama was now sleeping most of the time. And we all took turns taking care of her. Papa prayed earnestly every morning and night, but not even his prayers were of much help. She was too weak. Only a few short days after she came home, Mama died in her bed."

After her death Moshe Goldfarb was suddenly left with seven children: five boys and two girls. Simon was the youngest. Ester found herself thrust into a new and extremely difficult role. "I'm going to be your mother now," she bravely told all of them as they gathered around her. "And I promise that I'll do the best I can. But I'll need all of your help. I'm counting on everyone."

Brucha quickly became Ester's right hand, gladly helping with all the family chores. The pretty young girl was no longer able to study and read, the things she loved most. Brucha even lost the luxury of childhood, although she wasn't quite ready yet to become a woman.

Concealing her own grief over the loss of Mama, Ester, with Brucha's help, encouraged the family to continue to function as normally as possible. Right up to this very day.

"So now you know everything there is to know," said Aron at last.

Simon sat quietly weeping; he wiped his nose with his sleeve, trying his utmost to act as grown up as he could.

Aron rose from the grass, looked down at Simon and offered his extended hand. Simon grasped it eagerly as they made their way down the hill towards their home. A galaxy of bright stars silhouetted the small cottage. "Come on, little brother, it's time to go inside."

They stopped speaking about Mama.

The sudden noise made Ester rush to the shutter. She opened it slightly, Brucha stood beside her, her slender hand at her throat. Grim uniformed soldiers were banging loudly on the door of the house directly across the street. Aron peered through the shutter slats.

"Come quick, Papa!" he called. The Germans are coming for Mr. Met!"

Moshe Goldfarb hurriedly rushed his two daughters away and watched intently from the corner of the window.

The door across the street finally opened, and Moshe's Christian friend was shoved roughly aside as several soldiers entered his small cottage. Mr. Met stood in the door's frame, yellow light in the background. Two rifle-bearing sentries stood at either side of the doorway, erect and serious.

A covered jeep pulled up in front of the house, brakes screeching. A tall SS officer jumped out of the vehicle and gruffly barked commands at the sentries.

They snapped to attention and saluted. The officer confronted Mr. Met and spoke harshly to him.

"I think they've come for him, Papa," cried Aron. "I think they're going to take him away." Aron shuffled nervously over the thick white sand that served as a carpet across the bare wooden floor.

"Hush," Moshe admonished sternly.

Aron's father listened carefully to the muffled conversation. They were speaking in German, a language Moshe understood perfectly. During the Great War twenty years earlier, he and his best friend, Laibesz Kupke, served in the army together as translators. They spent several years among German-speaking soldiers.

"What are they saying to him?" asked Aron.

His father put a finger to Aron's lips, quieting him.

Aron's heart was pounding so loudly, he was certain everyone could hear. He balled his hands into fists.

Why Mr. Met? What had the kindly Christian done to be intruded upon so late at night? Aron had known this man for almost all of his life. As a small boy, Mr. Met would frequently invite him into his house. He would offer his young guest candy, sometimes placing him on his knee and regale him with stories about the wild animals of the forests. It didn't much matter to Aron that his tales were improvised, nor that his neighbor would usually repeat the same story over and over again. He had learned to respect this aging friend of his father. Indeed, he would often think of him as a sort of grandfather. A relative.

The officer shouted something to his men inside the house. After some long moments three soldiers came back out, reporting their findings, and shaking their

24

heads. It seemed obvious that whatever they were searching for, wasn't found. The SS officer took out his pistol, pointed it at the Pole, then demanded a reply to another question.

Aron knew that Met was frightened. He answered to the best of his ability. This was a proud man, not easily cowed. He was proud of his heritage, his country, Poland, and scornful of their unwelcome occupiers. Hadn't it been enough that the Germans had already looted the town of nearly everything it had?

Dignity, though, was the one possession they could never take away from him. Mr. Met continued to respond to the officer's questions in his halting German. Sometimes the long-faced SS man seemed content with his answers, other times not.

The conversation went on for what seemed to be an eternity. Actually only minutes had passed. Then, as abruptly as they had come, satisfied or not, the Germans suddenly left.

Mr. Met held his position in the doorway, looking on. He wiped perspiration from his brow, and remained there glaring contemptuously at his unwelcome visitors.

The SS officer paid no attention to him. He brushed mud from his leather boots with a handkerchief while his driver opened the jeep door. Then they sped away down a dark street. Total silence prevailed.

"They're not going to arrest him after all," Aron said jubilantly.

"Thank God for that," muttered Brucha.

Moshe heaved a sigh of relief. "Close the shutter, Aron," he said. "Close it tightly."

"What did the Nazis want?"

Moshe Goldfarb made no attempt to answer his son's question. He walked slowly over the dusty shelf containing his books, removed one and opened it to read.

Aron stood there impatiently. "Aren't you going to tell us anything?" he protested.

Moshe regarded his son as though he had no diea about what he was talking.

"None of this was important," he said brusquely. I want you to go to bed. It's getting late. You have to go to work early, and you need your rest."

There was no use in asking again, Aron realized. His father was going to remain tight-lipped and unwilling to discuss the incident. But the sinking feeling in his gut indicated to the young man that his father was hiding something from them.

Perhaps Papa didn't quite know what the commotion had been about. Had the Nazis suspected that Mr. Met was guilty of harboring someone?, Aron wondered. It was well known that Polish partisans were hiding out in the nearby forests. Or maybe Mr. Met was being accused of arousing unrest in Bialobrzegi.

Anything was possible. The Germans were always on the lookout for spies and saboteurs. Various individuals and groups were known to be unwilling to accept the new order imposed by the Third *Reich*. Armed citizens who ambushed patrols and detonated explosives along the rail lines, followers of Stalin. Communists, they were usually called. The greatest threat to Nazi supremacy, except for the Jews.

What Aron did know was that there was definitely a certain uneasiness about Papa's curt behavior that he recognized immediately. Was there a modicum of deep concern behind his outwardly calm facade?

"Brucha, turn off the lamp," Moshe snapped. "It's

time we all went to sleep." He rose, and put his worn book back on the shelf.

The girl quickly did as her father asked. The cottage was once again enveloped in darkness.

Aron knew, that for Papa, this night was not going to pass uneventfully.

Chapter Three

Once again he lay awake in his bed, his thoughts diffused. At least tonight Simon slept soundly, allowing Aron the freedom to contemplate. He was discouraged and confused.

How long could things go on this way, he asked himself. The German night invasion of his neighbor's house had shaken him more than he was willing to admit. Why wouldn't Papa listen to him, to his warnings? They could expect only disaster. Why did Papa so adamantly insist on remaining in Bialobrzegi, when, at least to Aron, the eventual outcome and fate of all the Jews was so apparent? They were already all prisoners *de facto* if not in name.

Aron raised his head and regarded his sleeping father. He brushed his fingertips through his hair.

You still believe in the innate goodness of man, don't you, Papa? You still think that people can be redeemed, that sooner or later, somehow, if your faith is strong enough, even the savage Nazis will come to their senses?

Deep down inside Aron wished he too could believe in Papa's way. It would have made life so much simpler. Had he been more like Jacob, a youth of ideals and progressive political beliefs, a socialist, courageous in his opinions, then perhaps the antagonists would be more clearly defined. Socialist against fascist. Jew against Nazi. Good against evil.

It wasn't that simple, though, nor would it ever be. It certainly had never been for him.

Aron was seven years old when he was enrolled in public school. By the time he reached the age of twelve his whole life was planned out for him, without his having any say in the matter. One night after supper, Papa took him aside for a man to man talk. "Aron, the time has come for us to decide what to do about your future," Papa said.

Aron listened dutifully as Papa's plans for him were spelled out.

"You're growing quickly, and I need you to help out in the family. You'll have to stop going to school and learn a trade."

There were no objections from the young man. That was the way of things in Poland, and most of Europe, for boys during those formative years. The father of the house decides his son's trade, the child becomes apprenticed to a selected craft. As it was with his three older brothers, so would it be with Aron. He understood what was expected of him and was willing to abide by his father's plan. If he wasn't going to attend the university, then Aron had hoped to find some future for himself in business. He didn't know exactly how, but he was certain he'd be able to do well. Those dreams were about to end.

29

"I've entered into an agreement with Barak," Moshe went on. "he's willing to take you in as a helper and teach you his trade."

Barak Bentu was a shoemaker. This certainly was not what Aron had planned for himself, and Papa knew this very well. Aron spoke his mind to his father without hesitation.

Moshe leaned back and heaved a long sign. "I know how you feel, Aron, I do know. But the family is counting on you. *I'm* counting on you. You know that I would never force you into anything unless there was no choice . . ."

"I understand that, Papa."

"Then learn to be a shoemaker for now, and later you can choose something else. Whatever you like."

Barak Bentu lived in a cottage by the river, in the shadow of the town's pride, the new bridge. The house consisted of two rooms—one upstairs for living purposes and one below, the workship where he fashioned his shoes and boots. To Aron's way of thinking Barak even looked the stereotype of a shoemaker. He was a bald and husky man, with shoulders that stooped from hunching over his bench all day. Barak already had one apprentice working for him; a crippled fellow with one leg so crooked that he was forced to wear special shoes. Aron now became the junior apprentice in the tiny establishment.

Each morning at eight, Aron responsibly went to Barak Bentu's house and worked until seven or eight in the evening. Mostly, his work consisted of running errands, cleaning up the shop and house, and generally doing exactly what Barak instructed him to do. For three years Aron toiled six days a week, and his father was given his meager wages. This was the arrangement. The contract made between the rabbi and the shoemaker, assuring that Aron would learn a trade, a skill that would be his for the rest of his life. For the Jewish holidays Barak sometimes gave Aron a pair of shoes as a gift. At other times he would receive a small bonus. However, Aron had no say in any of these matters.

Moshe Goldfarb had not wished to push his son into a life that he did not want. Nevertheless, there were seven children in the house, and Moshe was already doing as much as he could on his own to support them. There were times when Moshe had only enough money to buy a single loaf of bread. He would cut it into seven pieces, and distribute one portion to each of his hungry children.

"But you left nothing for yourself," Aron, Brucha or Ester would object.

The rabbi would quietly reply, "I ate, I ate. Don't worry so much about me." In truth, Papa had eaten nothing at all. As always, he sacrificed everything for his family.

Comparatively speaking, Barak Bentu was a wealthy man indeed. It seems that the shoemaker and his family were eating all day long. When Aron arrived for work, they were having breakfast, and while Aron ran his errands and learned his trade the family ate their lunch, and later their dinner. Aron would watch them with wide eyes and a growling hunger. He would stare at the pot of hot soup as its contents simmered on the stove, looked on with envy at the plates being filled with meat, potatoes, and noodles, and also pitchers of milk. Never once in all of his experiences, though, had Aron been invited to sit at the table and share a meal.

There was an old saying, that Aron kept repeating to himself, "When somebody has enough food, they can't believe that another is hungry."

Sometimes Aron's hunger was so great that when

Barak's wife went out to the market he would sneak into the kitchen and steal a slice of bread. Sometimes out of a need for food and sheer despair, he would come home and go directly to bed, crying into his pillow so no one would hear. He never told Papa any of this. It would only increase the hurt of the proud rabbi. A poor and devoutly pious man, Moshe had taught his family never to hate or be jealous of the good fortune of others. This was life, with all of its stark realities, and that was the way it was.

When Aron reached the age of fifteen his contract with Barak Bentu was fulfilled. It meant freedom for him at long last. The freedom for which he had been waiting. He knew he was not the most proficient of shoemakers, but he had learned his trade well enough. He had learned to take the raw materials along with a wooden form, then mold, cut, and nail the leather pieces together. Add a little polish, laces, and there you had it—a new pair of shoes.

Shortly after, Papa found a new job for him with a Jewish shoe manufacturer in town named Ume Gutowicz. His new employer conducted a small business almost singlehandedly, producing far better quality footwear than did Barak. Together with Ume Gutowicz's son, Aron began to work at his new trade in earnest. This time the arranged contracts were for only six month periods, and since he was now fifteen years old—an imminent precursor of young manhood —Aron even got to keep a little of the money he earned after turning over his pay to Papa.

Skilled, hard-working, he enjoyed his employment by Ume. He took pride and satisfaction in his work for the first time. Moreover, the money he was earning was a great help to his family. Still, even as he sat at his small bench with tools in hand, wearing his apron, he dreamed of the day when he would make his own decisions. The time Papa had foretold, when he might decide for himself what he wanted to do in the future.

It was while working there for Ume Gutowicz that his hopes and dreams suddenly, inexplicably, came to a crashing halt.

It was September of 1939.

A sudden loud ear-shattering blast shook the small workshop's foundations. Aron and the others scurried to the door to learn what had happened.

To his dismay, many people were running in the street, screaming. Smoke billowed high into the sky everywhere. Warplanes shrieked overhead, bombs whistling as they fell.

Buildings were crushed, reduced to rubble. The *Luftwaffe* now dominated the skies. The Third *Reich* was bombing Bialobrzegi.

Thus, at the age of fifteen, Aron realized that Poland was on the verge of total disaster. The war had begun less than a month before, and the people of Bialobrzegi would huddle and listen to the news being broadcast over one of the few radios available. Poland's situation was worsening. Warsaw had been under siege. The government and army were fleeing. They knew that the German Army was coming closer. One did not need to be told or have to read about it—the audible sounds of the bombs was proof enough.

"Go home, Aron," Ume Gutowicz gravely told his sturdy young worker. Aron set down his tools and ran out into the street.

Black billows of thick smoke enveloped the beautiful bridge he had so dearly loved. The great structure had been reduced to masses of smashed concrete and twisted steel. German trucks and motorcycles rumbled speedily through the town square and along the

33

myriad of winding streets. Aghast, Aron saw a neighbor, the ten-year old son of another rabbi, Laibesz Kucie, scramble and dodge to get out of the way of the racing vehicles.

The lad was evidently not fast enough. The front of a truck smashed into the child, hurling him high like a rag doll. The boy hit the ground with terrible force. Then again and again the truck wheels rolled over the already broken bones, leaving in the middle of the street a blood-soaked, lifeless mangled body. This scene seared his impressionable sensitive soul like a branding iron, indelibly etching in his mind a permanent image so horrible, its nightmare haunted him ceaselessly.

The German soldiers claimed that the incident was an accident. Aron and others knew better. The boy had been wearing a *yarmulka*, a Jewish religious skullcap, so the Germans plainly saw that he was a Jew. They had purposefully run him down. Murdered him, and left him there lying in his own blood.

Aron had spent a great deal of time with his friends discussing what might happen next. Poland's armed opposition to Germany's invasion was lost; born in Poland, schooled in Poland, reading and writing perfect Polish, his initial concern was for his conquered nation. They wondered what the occupying invader might do to them next. These were his primary apprehensions. Neither he nor many others imagined that the Jews of Poland were to be singled out for terrorization and murder.

This belief was quickly disabused.

Only days after the death of the rabbi's young son, German soldiers pulled into the square with a truck. They began to distribute loaves of bread to the people of the town.

While he stood in line waiting his turn, some of the Polish people started to point at him, angrily shouting, "*Juda. Juda.* Jew. Jew." The soldiers pulled him from the line and refused him any bread.

Aron was bewildered. What had he done wrong? Why was he being singled out this way? He was no different from any other citizen of Bialobrzegi. Or was he?

"Don't you know why they threw you out of the bread line, Aron?" a Jewish neighbor asked him afterwards. He realized, for perhaps the first time, how naive he'd been.

It was only then that he heard about the grand plan of the Third *Reich*; *Führer* Hitler's agenda for destroying the Jewish people once and for all. Years before in Hitler's infamous *Mein Kampf*, he exhorted and ordered that war was to be waged against all Jews. Not just those in Germany, or Poland, but in all of Europe. Jews were vermin, Hitler proclaimed. Jews were parasites, evil. Communists. Corruptors of Civilization, the mortal enemy of every good Christian. Jews were the cause of all of Germany's difficulties. Hate them. Beat them. *Kill them.*

The very idea of this brutal and inhuman resolution was so staggering, so unbelievable, it left him stunned and reeling. As with Papa, he couldn't find a way to come to terms with such a barbaric philosophy. What sane person could?

Why would Hitler want to do such a thing? For what reasons? What wrong had Aron done to anyone? What crimes had the Jews committed? Papa had worked hard all of his life to support his family. He was a decent man with quite a number of Christian friends; a respectable individual who had never hurt anyone. All he ever wanted was to see his children grow up and lead productive lives. Yet, because of their religious beliefs Jews were to be herded apart from all others and condemned.

Why? Always the same nagging question: *Why?*

During the first few weeks after the invasion Aron discussed this issue daily with his friends. Soon, though, the German military command decreed in Bialobrzegi that no Jews were permitted to gather in groups and speak—no matter what the reason. Any infraction of this order would subject the transgressor to immediate arrest. Even those who gathered in their own homes faced incarceration. No questions, and no explanations. Anyone who dared challenge this authority ran the risk of being shot.

Soon the Nazis were issuing all kinds of new and outrageous regulations; one of the first of these was that Jews were required to work without pay. In Bialobrzegi—as in all of Poland's towns—the Germans helped to set up special Jewish committees to supply laborers for them. Jews were now selecting the forced laborers.

Members of the dreaded SS arrived. They occupied a large farm that once belonged to a Polish prince named Glinka. It encompassed thousands of acres of good land, along with horses, cows, and many crops. Each day the newly formed 'Jewish Committee' was ordered to assign between fifty and one hundred people to this nearby farm. Three kilometers from Bialobrzegi, it was known as Sucha.

Those who had some money would pay poorer folk like Aron and his older brothers to report for work in their stead. Sometimes Aron was sent into the fields that surrounded the great estate itself. Prince Glinka's palace. He was frequently assigned to the vegetable garden or the greenhouse. He served as water carrier, pushing barrels to the wagons, or cleaning the estate's

36

roadways. At other times he would chop wood for the magnificent fireplaces of the grand house, so that the SS elite could keep cozy and warm during the cold winter nights.

The aristocrats of Sucha had maintained their estate for longer than anyone could remember. Aron had never once been permitted entry inside those great walls until one day he was sent to assist in its cleaning, and to help pack some items for shipment to Berlin.

As he entered the palace, he was awe-struck by its splendor. It was reminiscent of a fairy tale book. Huge crystal chandeliers hung from the high ceilings, reflectively dazzling in the light. Lush and thickly woven carpets spread across the freshly polished floors. There were knives, forks, silver spoons, and plates made of pure gold, hand-woven tapestries decorating the walls. It was an incredible display of wealth. Prosperity beyond a poor village boy's power to imagine. He was amazed at the magnitude of opulence at Sucha.

The Germans, though, had their own plans for Prince Glinka's remaining wealth. Everything of value was boxed and readied for loading, and the Germans had it hauled away. Removed forever and into their private collections, plundering Poland of its once royal heritage.

Aron and his brothers became such regular workers at Sucha that the soldiers recognized and got to know them personally. The brothers would leave home for the estate at seven in the morning, walking in a line of a hundred others, guarded by armed police. They would work until eight at night, when the police escort reversed the morning procedure and marched the forced laborers back to town. Once in a while, Aron would hide a few tomatoes or potatoes inside his pants or shirt and bring them home. It was his small contribution towards his family's survival. However as time passed this became a very dangerous thing for him to do. A serious, punishable crime.

The Germans began tightening the reins on the Jewish people. Every day new announcements in Polish were being posted in the streets, listing new and stricter restrictions.

Jews were no longer permitted to shop in the same stores that the Polish Christians did.

Jewish children were no longer allowed to attend school; nor would they be permitted to leave their homes after eight in the evening.

They were now ordered to wear yellow armbands bearing the Star of David.

Humiliation after humiliation was heaped upon the Jews, and indignities were everyday occurrences for them.

If a Jew did not have a special pass certifying that he was in the employ of the Germans, he was no longer permitted to leave the confines of the town. If one tried to leave—and was caught—Nazi justice was unrelenting: immediate death.

One young girl whom Aron recalled from the neighboring village of Grujec, was sent out by her desperate family to bring back some food from the recently harvested tracts. As the pathetic youngster scrounged for a few potatoes in the field, a soldier whom Aron knew named Willie aimed his rifle and killed her on the spot. Hidden inside her bloody dress were her meager stolen foods. A few carrots and a handful of potatoes. For that munificent feast she paid with her life.

This was Nazi justice.

It was during 1941, two years after the invasion, that Jews began to be herded from other towns between Warsaw and Radom into Bialobrzegi. A few hundred from this vicinity, five hundred from some other

38

village. Long lines of haggard, confused citizens of Poland—all of them sharing only one thing in common, their religion, came pouring into the town. The healthy as well as the sick. The young and the old. Mothers with small children clutching their hands, men dragging sacks containing their entire possessions. Elderly couples pushing hand carts over the bumpy dirt roads. In heat and in rain. In cold and in snow. An endless progression of demoralized humanity.

Sometimes they prayed, they cried, at times they were silent in their bewilderment. Uprooted and homeless, shouted at by their watchful guards, treated ignobly without a scintilla of respect.

Ten thousand Jews were crammed into the scenic town of Bialobrzegi. Ten thousand hapless souls with no place to live, no jobs, and very little food. As many as forty people were sometimes forced to share a single room for shelter. Everyday some died from typhus and starvation.

Between the city of Radom to the south, and Warsaw in the north, for fifty to one hundred kilometers around the town, the countryside was *Judenrein*—free of Jews. Bialobrzegi had become a ghetto.

Aron knew he was far luckier than most; he did have work. When not toiling in the fields at Sucha he was a laborer for the military police. He shined the boots of the German officers, chopped wood for their fireplaces so they would be comfortable during the long freezing winter nights. He saw, at first hand, what the Nazis were doing. Watched them drag Jews to their headquarters and beat them. Then, take them out at night and kill them.

It was sadistic and barbaric, surreal and unbelievable. Yet this was no dream, no fantasy, Aron knew. This was a nightmare come true. And he was a witness.

As with Moshe Goldfarb, most orthodox Jewish men

wore beards in the customary tradition. The military police would often haul such Jews into custody and cut off their beards. Then they would laugh. Aron found himself in the untenable position of seeing this happen, but helpless to stop them. Had he tried, they would have had their brutal sport with him as well. Dying would do no good nor serve any purpose.

Working for the military was a horrible job. To serve these thugs and behave as though the atrocities weren't happening or had no meaning, was insufferable.

It was a matter of survival; Aron's own, and his family's. Since Moshe was not permitted to teach religious lessons any longer, or even to work for pay, the only monies coming into the household was the pittance Aron, Yitzhak and Abe could earn. Papa rarely even left the house anymore. He kept studying the bible, and continuing to pray.

As the days passed, the soldiers became bolder and more brutal. In the headquarters' backyard they built what they referred to as a 'special room'. A windowless, dark dungeon-like cell, into which Jews were locked along with three starved German shepherd dogs. They would viciously attack. Screams could be heard quite often. It made Aron shudder. Again, he pretended that he didn't see or know what was taking place.

He was frightened. He would come home and find that he was unable to sleep. Or worse, reliving the nightmarish sufferings of those his torturers had condemned. Ester listened as he recounted these events to her, but his father could not bring himself to believe that the Germans would do anything like that. He remembered them from the days of the Great War.

"When I was in the Army the Germans were good to the Jewish people," he would proclaim. "This cannot be. They would not—could not—do these terrible things."

"Papa, it's *true*! I've seen it with my own eyes."

To which Moshe replied, "Why should Germans be any different today from what they were twenty-five years ago?"

But this was no longer the world of 1914. This was 1941. And the rabbi could not really understand this new world in which they were living. Aron realized that his father was making a mistake. A terrible one.

Not too many days later Moshe was talking outside with several neighbors. A passing soldier stopped and stared at him.

"Jew, you have a fine red beard," he shouted.

Then he and several comrades walked up to the rabbi and seized him. The soldier scornfully took out a pair of scissors and publicly humiliated the man. After they were done they methodically made their way along the entire street, cutting off the beards of all the men they found.

That evening, in the yellow light of the kerosene lamp, the family huddled and cried. They cried for Papa's degradation that deprived him of the symbol of his religion, leaving him nothing save the little dignity he valiantly tried to display.

Bastards, Aron cursed.

Once again he steeled his resolve. If there was a way—any way—he would find it.

The Jews of the overflowing ghetto had no one to help them organize against these ever multiplying outrages. Systematically, the Nazis had succeeded in eliminating all of the Jewish leaders. Each night it had been different ones: several prominent doctors, a number of lawyers, and educators. All murdered. People's fright increased. New and even worse edicts were summarily issued.

Any Jew caught disobeying the military laws will find not only himself accountable, but his entire family as well. They will all be punished.

Like Moshe, most Jews did not really believe something like this could happen. Certainly not to the innocents, small children, old men, young mothers who were machine gunned for the slightest infraction.

Even more unbelievable to the ghetto community was the fact that the Polish people themselves—their neighbors for all their lives—were actually helping the invaders accomplish their dirty work. When many Poles found a runaway Jew they would turn them in to the Nazi police, often in exchange for little more than some sugar or a bottle of vodka.

Yitzhak and Abe were virtual prisoners on their jobs at Sucha. The SS men had selected their hundred young workers well. They were hand picked: Strong, virile youths particularly skillful in the special trades that were needed.

Aron knew that Yitzhak was well-liked because he was such a fine worker. They assigned him inside the Sucha estate walls as a handyman.

Aron's own work was now on the power line. A truck picked up the workers from town, cramming in as many as possible, for the work site. On one recent morning eighty laborers were jammed into that truck. During the arduous trip through a tiny village, a cow ran onto the narrow road. The driver lost control as he tried to swerve the vehicle. The truck flipped over on its side. Aron had managed to jump free. Many of his co-workers were crushed beneath the vehicle, others were badly injured.

42

Accompanying soldiers came running to the accident site.

"Who are these boys?" one soldier asked.

By this time Aron spoke and understood German quite well, and he listened with abject horror as the other soldier answered, "Just Jews. We're going to wipe them off the face of the earth soon, anyway."

Aron was aghast. he repeated every word to his family and friends. It didn't matter, though. Rumors were already rife. Everyone already knew it might happen at anytime. If not tonight, then tomorrow; whenever it pleased them. The Jews were helpless. They were trapped like cattle, penned in by barbed wire fences with no way out.

All Jews, it was said, were going to be relocated to so-called work camps. Camps that contained huge smokestacks and poison gas.

These were designed to achieve the total destruction of the Jewish people.

In his bed, Aron lay tormented. Restlessly he tossed and turned. And he fully realized that the worst had not even begun.

Chapter Four

"**R**aus! *Raus!*" They were shouting. "Out! Out!"

Rifles were being shot into the air. Trucks and jeeps fanning out from the square in a shadowy procession as the first light of dawn spread over the town.

Yelling filled the streets, soldiers' boots beat hard on the cobblestone. Butts of rifles pounded against doors.

"Get up! Get up! All of you! Get out of your houses!"

Aron jumped from the bed with a start. Ester was already standing by the window, little Simon quivered as he remained at her side.

"It's come," Aron muttered lowly.

His frightened eyes met Papa's. "You know we have to do as they say . . ."

Moshe Goldfarb nodded gloomily. He picked up his small bundle of clothing.

"The murderers are here," he said.

Aron swung the door open. Neighbors were already in the street, their own pitiable bundles under their arms. Germans and Ukrainians with machine guns kept steady, unblinking eyes on the enemy they had come to conquer; the "enemy" of unarmed men, mothers and children.

"Papa, please, don't let them take us away," cried Ester. Her shoulders shook as she covered her face with both hands and started to sob. Moshe held her close in an effort to console his eldest daughter.

Simon's trembling hands took hold of Aron's and Papa's. Tears were streaming down his face as they stepped outside. Confusion was everywhere.

A soldier malevolently motioned with the barrel of his rifle at the sad little family. "Move it, move it," he barked. "Get in line with the others."

Ester clutched her bundle to her breast. She stumbled on the stones.

All around them moved a horde of tormented souls. People being herded, pushed, and threatened. "Over there, over there," the soldiers shouted, but where they meant for the mass of bewildered humanity to go, no one seemed to know.

"Stay together," said Moshe above the din. "Everyone hold hands." They started to march with the flow.

The unexpected burst of machine gun fire sent the crowd screaming and racing in all directions. Hails of bullets pinged into the crowd. Men, women and children staggered and fell, bleeding.

"Run, Papa!" cried Aron.

In a frantic effort, Moshe took hold of his daughters and Simon and desperately tried to make his way down the street. Aron was right alongside them, when suddenly a man dropped to his knees right in front of him. One hand clutched his belly, the other grasped

45

frenziedly into the air. Blood gushed between his fingers. His eyes were wide and wild, filled with terror. Aron saw his agony, his silent plea for help. Then, without a word, he collapsed.

Now others were being hit. One here, one there. Then more and more. It was carnage. People screaming with all of their fading might for someone to help them. Moaning as they staggered and fell, laying still in the gutters, faces contorted with pain and tears, and still the rat, tat tat of machine gun fire continued.

Everyone ran in all directions. Aron gasped. Not more than twenty feet in front of him stood pretty Rachel Weisbord, the fifteen-year old beauty he had always admired. He wanted to call to her, to tell her to wait for him. But Rachel was running as fast as she could, her long blond hair bouncing in the warm wind.

Aron cried out in despair. He saw the gray-green uniform of the soldier as he kneeled and leveled his machine gun. Then cold-bloodedly he squeezed the trigger. A burst of bullets sprayed Rachel. The young girl slumped to the ground while the mindless crowd trampled over her bloody corpse.

Numbed, dazed and reeling, Aron was pushed senselessly along with the throng. Like a lost mob, the wretched temporary survivors raced through the narrow streets of the ghetto. Past the wooden cottages, over the dirt roads and the cobblestones. All about him people continued to collapse.

His eyes searched in frenzy for his family. He couldn't see any of them.

Had Papa been killed? Ester? Simon? Aron didn't know what to think or do. There was no way to reach them. His ears were filled with the constant crackle of deadly gunfire seemingly coming from everywhere, and followed by the ghastly shrieks of the wounded and dying after every burst.

Soldiers joined the attack wielding sticks; they beat some of them while stopping to shoot others. Why this happened he didn't know. He only knew that the terror was like nothing he had ever imagined.

People were being herded like cattle this way and that, being led to slaughter, ever closer to the vast marketplace on the edge of town.

"Keep going!" the soldiers were shouting at those still alive. In a daze they obeyed.

Those moving too slowly were smashed on the back or head with military nightsticks. More people fell, especially the old, unable to keep up with the torturous rapid pace.

At last Aron reached the marketplace. There the Jews of the ghetto were being crammed together as rings of soldiers surrounded them with drawn weapons. Thousands of victims, massed in a single group, bloodied, helpless, some scantily dressed, some in their nightshirts, still others clutching their carefully prepared bundles. Aron scanned this agglomeration of squalid humanity in the hope of seeing his family. There were too many people, though; far too many. He had no idea where to start to look.

"Aron! Here! Here!"

He turned at the faint sound of his name. But all he could see was a host of shabby, pitiful souls. All he could hear were their sobs and moans.

"Here we are, Aron!"

It was Ester's voice!

Aron fought his way through the wailing crowd, as his name rang in his ears. Suddenly, there they were. Tears were streaming down their faces. Except for his and Papa's. In turn Aron hugged them all.

A German soldier started screaming at them above the noise. To gain their attention he fired his rifle into the air. Now the throng quickly quieted, waiting for his dreaded announcement.

"Anyone who works on the powerline at Zoerk, show me your papers!" he called. "Hold them high in the air!"

Moshe looked over at his son. His eyes were more revealing than his words, "You have your papers, Aron. Show them."

"But, Papa—"

"Those with papers stand by the stables!" shouted the soldier.

Aron didn't know what to do. He looked about perplexed. His documents were in his possession, but showing them would mean separating himself from his family.

"Go, my son," said Moshe Goldfarb. "Do as they say."

It was a lovely autumn morning, the sky, deep blue, the birds chirping in the trees. Sunlight beamed over the gathering of human misery in the Bialobrzegi marketplace. It glinted off the brass decorations on the soldiers' uniforms. It shined over the faces of the dead lying motionless on the soil.

"But Papa. . . ."

Moshe realized at last that this was the end for them. He had been wrong. His desperate hopes had been dashed. He was a good and kind man, a man who had lived a hard life struggling to raise his family in the proper way. And now, amid the carnage and evil that befell them, he realized that one of his children had a chance to survive.

He held out his arms and placed his strong hands on Aron's head, staring deeply into the youth's eyes. His face was filled with the same agony and torment that prevailed among the dying and the doomed. He wanted his son to be with him, but even more fervently, he wished his son to live.

Aron had never disobeyed his father. Not even now. "All right, Papa," he whispered.

He went to his younger sister, bent slightly, and held Brucha close to him. The girl's long red hair glinted in the sunlight.

"Listen to everything Papa and Ester tell you," he said.

His sister nodded, fighting back tears. He kissed her.

Standing up straight, he looked forlornly at Ester, the girl who had become the mother of the house. The one who was the catalyst in holding everything together over these last few years, no matter how impossible the circumstances seemed. She met his tearful gaze. "Goodbye, Ester. . . . My sister."

She choked back her own emotions. "Aron . . . God bless. . . ."

Kneeling, he took young Simon in his arms. He had no words for him. What could he possibly say? Instead he hugged the boy as tightly as he could. Simon's eyes were shut, tears falling under his eyelashes and coursing down his round cheeks. Aron wiped away the tears.

Turning lastly to Papa, he managed to speak. "God help us to live through this catastrophe and bring us together again."

Moshe squeezed Aron strongly, rocking back and forth as he kissed him. He looked deeply into Aron's face. His expressive eyes were dry, but his voice was filled with tenderness and affection. "Go, my son," he said, "Maybe you will survive."

Aron nodded, aware of what Papa wanted, knowing what must be done.

He held the precious powerline document above his head, and pushed his way towards the stables. He'd walked no more than a few meters when he stopped abruptly. He'd had so many opportunities to escape, he knew, so many other chances to flee into the forests. Not once had he tried. Not out of fear but because of his need to be close to his family. At this moment he asked himself why it should now be different than it was before. Whatever their fate, it would be his also. They shared everything together, as a family. He turned around and started to go back.

A soldier saw him and struck him vehemently on the back with his club.

"You don't belong back there," he shouted at the youth. "That's the wrong line. You have your papers. Go over to the stables."

Aron did as he was ordered.

When he finally glanced back, his family was lost in the huge crowd. Something deep inside gnawed at him until it hurt more than the club ever could.

He knew somehow that he would never see any of them again.

Part Two

Part Two

Chapter Five

About 200 young men had been selected to work for the Germans on the militarily valuable Zoerk power-line. Aron searched the faces of those around him. They were anxious, fearful faces, not unlike his own. Some among the segregated group were crying, others were visibly shaking. The majority, like Aron, stood mute and staring, attempting to seek out their families before they were taken away.

Across the square, at the marketplace, stood those thousands waiting to be transferred from the town to a new, unknown destination. Their faces seemed drawn, stricken, and devoid of emotion. The blood from those who were slain during the massacre was splattered at their feet, over the cobblestone, and the clothing of the dispossessed. With glazed eyes they stood silently staring out into the distance but behaving as though they could see nothing around them. They were the unwanted people of Poland, gathered together as farmers collect their sheep. They were fearful and bewildered people. Most acted as though they didn't realize what had happened this morning. They were suffering from shock, Aron knew. The grimness of the scene was accentuated by the wall of soldiers surrounding them with weapons in hand.

Aron felt shivers running down his spine.

These are the dead, he told himself as he surveyed the ghastly spectacle. *A living cemetery. The Jews—all of them—are going to die.*

No one in the assemblage beside the stables had any idea of what their fate would be. Perhaps the powerline workers who had been separated from their families were not going to be sent to work at all. They represented the youngest and strongest of the group. The most capable fomenters of a possible rebellion. Maybe the Germans had secretly planned to murder them first to rid Bialobrzegi of its most virile youth.

A stone-faced SS officer spoke with several of the rifle-bearing guards. After he'd given his instructions, orders were shouted.

"This group move!" A few soldiers indicated the way with rifle butts.

Heads were bowed, the powerline workers were marched away in a line, back into the town and through the narrow streets of the now emptied ghetto. Horse-drawn wagons lined both sides of the streets. Corpses were piled one on top of another and were so loaded down that the horses had to strain to pull the wagons.

It was apparent to Aron that the Nazis had made careful preparations for this morning's butchery. Taking the ghetto by surprise, quietly and unexpectedly, efficiently minimizing the possibility of the Jews fighting back.

The Christian Poles, meanwhile, had been conspicuously absent in the streets during the awful bloodbath. They remained behind closed shutters and locked doors, safe within their homes. As the labor gang passed row after row of unscathed houses it became quite apparent that the military authorities had warned them to remain inside, and warned them not to venture outside at the risk of losing their lives.

Aron grimaced at this realization. His thin face choleric, his calloused hands balled into tight fists. He wanted to strike back. Lash out in some way and kill at least one of his captors. Hate raged through him like wildfire. It took maximum restraint for him to hide his true emotions. To walk in silence with the others, maintaining his calm and resolve, and to obey all the orders he was given. This much he had to do in order to survive.

Were Bialobrzegi's Christian Poles quietly laughing at the rag-tag group of Jews being marched through the winding streets? He was sure many of them were. The Koszlas of this world. The Jew-haters. Those who served their Nazi masters well, like mangy dogs waiting for a reward.

Aron kept telling himself that he must somehow live through this day, escape this mindless extermination. His head was reeling, and with side glances he looked intently at the faces of the accompanying soldiers, remembering as many of them as he could for the time when his turn came.

Revenge would be his, someday.

Someday.

He repeated the word over and over. Through all of his torment it was all that kept him going.

At length, the work gang was halted, divided, and placed inside a row of emptied houses. Mutely they waited while the burial details went about their grisly task of disposing of the bodies.

"They killed almost three hundred today," someone said quietly.

Another young man nodded. "They're forcing the town's Jews to bury them."

Night fell. The workers sat disconsolately across the floor, waiting. After a time a few more Jews were brought in, escorted by soldiers.

"Sit with the others," they were told.

Aron's eyes widened. Among the new arrivals was Chaim Izon, an old friend. The two youths looked at one another but said nothing. Chaim found a place to sit near Aron. Then, they waited for the soldiers to leave.

Chaim's clothes were ragged and dirty. Aron noticed that his thick hands were caked with dried earth, and his shoes were muddy.

"What happened outside?" asked Aron.

"Shhh."

Chaim put a finger to his lips. His small eyes darted cat-like in the dark, seeking out possible informers. When he finally decided that it was safe to speak it was in a whisper. "The Poles were driving the wagons filled with the dead. They'd been waiting for hours to haul the bodies away. I think they were all recruited for this job yesterday."

"You mean they *knew* what was going to happen?"

"Of course they knew. At least the wagon drivers did."

Chaim shut his eyes; he leaned back and exhaled with a long sigh of fatigue. A worker's cap was tilted to one side over a shock of his dark hair. Exhaustion accentuated his haggard features. "They drove the bodies

56

far out to the field so no one could see what they were doing," he continued. "There was one huge mass grave which was dug for all of them. One large hole in the ground. It took about fifty people to dig that common grave, Aron. The Germans grouped around, watching. Then all the bodies were dumped into it. They covered the grave with dirt, and left. Not a single prayer was said over their corpses."

"How do you know all of this?" Aron demanded.

"How do *I* know?"

A single tear rolled down Chaim's thin face. He wiped it away with the side of his sleeve. "Oh, Aron. I know because I was there." He sat up straight and looked steadily into his friend's eyes. Aron felt cold as Chaim added, "I was one of the gravediggers."

The truck filled with workers drove the twenty five kilometers to the powerline. As they did on every other day, the laborers picked up their shovels and began to work. They would spend fourteen hours at the site, looking on while concrete was poured and more steel poles were set into the ground. Then they were herded back to the town, too weary to talk.

"Aron Goldfarb!" boomed the husky voice. "Look over here."

Startled, Aron turned. Standing amid the shadows of the workers' billet, beckoning to him, was one of his Christian neighbors.

Aron's mouth dropped. "Jan! Jan Jarzobek!" he called. Jan had been no friend to the Nazis, Aron knew. In recent days he had spent much of his time gathering information on the massacre and its survivors.

The Pole eased his way closer to the youngster. His face was sad as he looked at him.

"Have you found anything out for me?" Aron asked.

Jan placed his hand on Aron's shoulder. "Your

father, your sister, all of them—everyone was force-marched for hours. They were taken about forty kilometers from the town, I think. The railroad trains were waiting for them to be loaded. All the Jews were forced inside the cattle cars, to be taken away to a camp. . . ."

Aron clutched at his friend's sleeve. His eyes were pleading. "Everyone was taken to the railroad, Jan? Are you sure of that? *Everyone?*"

Jan nodded. "I'm sure. I saw them, Aron; with my own eyes. Your father was limping, so badly, he was barely able to walk. They were all helping him."

There was a lump in Aron's throat. "What did the Germans do to Papa?"

"I don't know. But they're gone, Aron. All of them, moved far from here. Now you have to be strong, boy. *Live.* It's what your father wanted." He squeezed Aron's arm. "You *must* survive."

"Thank you for telling me all this, Jan. . . ."

"Good luck, Aron. May God be with you."

As suddenly as he had appeared, the Christian was gone, back into the shadows of the night. Aron stood motionless. He didn't cry, he couldn't. He had already seen so much death, so much brutality, he would have to live with this and any other misfortunes that might come his way. It had to be done. Once more he buoyed his resolve. He would be strong indeed. As strong as necessary. Exactly as Jan had asked him to be.

He returned to his barrack, and as he fought to ease his highly charged emotional state he recalled Papa's last words to him, "Go, my son. Maybe you will survive." Aron looked up at the starry night sky.

I will, Papa. He promised aloud. *As sure as there is a God, I will.*

Aron always did as his father told him.

Chapter Six

"It's only a matter of time before they line us all up against a wall and shoot us," Chaim said in a hushed voice to those huddled around him.

"Shooting us would be an easy death," added Issac, another youth in the group. Stories of the infamous gas chambers being constructed and those already in operation were common knowledge.

Aron listened closely to the debates among his comrades. They all suffered fatigue from the fourteen hour days of hard labor, and malnutrition. All were being kept on a very fine line between existence and death. A line any SS soldier could obliterate at a whim.

"Make no mistake about it," said Chaim. "Right now they need us to work." He glanced around at the faces, singling them out one by one. "You, Aron, you, Jonathan. You have muscles they can put to productive use. Strong backs and strong arms. So do most of us." Somberly, he added, "But the day is approaching when we'll be finished on the powerline. Then what do you think they're going to do with us? Send us all home?"

"Maybe they will ship us out to another place," offered Issac. "And after that to somewhere else. We could be working like this for years."

Chaim laughed humorlessly at the suggestion. "Don't dream. And don't for a moment believe they'll keep us alive one extra minute longer than they must. We'll be killed eventually. Just as the rest."

"Chaim's right," said Aron after he thought about it. "Does anyone really believe they'll keep us alive indefinitely? Don't be stupid. We're already as good as dead. All of us."

"He's right," said someone else from the rear. "Why waste precious food and clothing on a bunch of Jews? After they killed my grandfather they stole his gold teeth, poured kerosene over his body and burned him to cinders. Why should they concern themselves with the likes of us?"

It was a point well taken. Every single young man working on the powerline had similar stories to tell. How relatives or friends had been killed in cold blood and then left as so much disposable trash. No, the Nazis would have no second thoughts about what to do with their laborers once their work was completed.

"So what do you recommend we do?"

Aron sighed, and addressed them all. "The only thing we can do is try to escape."

"Now *you're* the one who's dreaming," added another of the group named Jakob. "Have you forgotten what happened to Dov? He told us the same thing, said he was going to get away from here. But he didn't get very far did he?"

Everyone became silent. Dov, and several others in recent months, had slipped by the guards at night and made it out beyond the fields. Neither Dov nor any of the others had fled very far before they were caught. They were then brought back and executed publicly, but not after being brutally tortured for days. When Dov was hanged he was virtually carried to the gallows. His face had been beaten to a pulp. His nose was broken, and his jaw fractured. His eyes were so swollen, he couldn't open them. His ribs were cracked, and his fingers crushed. The SS had taken sadistic delight in punishing him before he was mercifully put to death. After so much unbearable torture, he must have welcomed the end.

The group sat brooding, deeply immersed in their own thoughts. Of course, Jakob was right. It was one thing to die—they had already lived with the threat of imminent death ever present—but having to suffer the severe brutality that preceded the final act was another matter to contemplate and dread.

It was Aron who finally broke the silence. "So what are we supposed to do? Should we all just give up and supinely wait for them to slay us? We're still human beings, aren't we? No matter what the Nazis say, we still have a right to live."

Chaim morosely replied, "You can take your chances and run if you so decide, Aron. It's your prerogative. But don't expect me to go along with you."

His friend Chaim wasn't totally wrong either, Aron realized. The odds weighed heavily against anyone escaping from the camp. The dogs would relentlessly hunt you down. The guards were quite eager to publicly exhibit another example of what happens to those who foolishly attempt to flee.

The Nazi noose, unfortunately, was already waiting to be placed around all their necks—and beginning to tighten.

"Goldfarb, get up and collect all your things."

Aron woke with a start. It was an early October Sunday morning in 1942. With blurry eyes he looked up at the soldier at the edge of his bunk. "What's the matter? What do you want me for? What did I do?"

The soldier did not answer, he just motioned for him to get out of bed and gather his bundle of clothes. Aron complied as quickly as he could.

Sunlight hurt his eyes as he stepped outside. A horse and cart were waiting, loaded with various crates and boxes.

"Get inside the wagon, Goldfarb," another guard barked.

"Why? Where are you taking me?"

"You're being removed from the powerline crew."

Removed?

His heart almost reached his throat. They didn't need him anymore. He was no longer of any use to them. They were going to take him out into the fields and shoot him.

"Removing me to where?" he asked in a shaky voice.

The soldier smiled wanly. "You must have very powerful friends, Goldfarb. We're transferring you. You're going back to work at that palace you loved so much. Back to Sucha."

Sucha? Was it possible? Were they really reassigning him to the great estate, or was this just a sop to stop him from putting up a fight?

Comparatively speaking, working at the castle had been an easy job. More important, though, Itzhak and Abe were still working at the palace. If the guard was telling him the truth, then he was going to be reunited with his brothers. It sounded almost too good to be true.

"I'll take charge of things now, corporal," came a strong, commanding voice from behind.

The soldier snapped to attention and saluted the approaching SS officer.

Aron stared in wonder. He recognized the man from his days in the prince's estate.

Oto Mairla was a captain in the dreaded SS. Young, slender, blond and blue-eyed; the prototype of a member of the Aryan race. He cut a commanding, authoritative figure, exactly like the ones featured in the Nazi propaganda posters.

"Get into the wagon, Aron," said the officer, gesturing impatiently with his hand.

Aron jumped inside without a word.

"Another Jew will be sent here to replace this one," the SS officer told the guard. The soldier nodded and saluted again as the captain climbed onto the wagon's buckboard. Oto Mairla raised his right hand. *"Heil Hitler!"*

The SS officer took the reins, tugged gently and the wagon began to roll. Aron looked back at the fading barracks. There had been no time to say goodbye to anyone. Nor had he any idea how this good fortune came to pass. But he did recall that Captain Oto Mairla of Sucha always had a high regard for him as a worker.

Goodbye, my friends, Chaim, Issac. Farewell, Jakob. Good luck to you all . . .

The ride took less than an hour. The wagon moved slowly through the tree-filled hills, along the old winding road. Soon the grand castle came in sight, and Aron became tense. He prayed that since he'd last seen his brothers, no serious harm had come to them. The thought of the three of them becoming reunited at last seemed almost too good to be true.

To enhance his great good fortune both Yitzhak and Abe, looking as well as when he'd last seen them, were eagerly awaiting his arrival.

"I don't understand any of this," Aron said after throwing his arms around his blond-haired brothers, greeting them with tears of joy.

Itzhak smiled broadly and impishly, his curly blond hair blowing in the autumn breeze.

Abe laughed aloud. His older siblings spoke over each other's voices as they welcomed Aron.

"I went to see Oto Mairla and personally pleaded with him, Abe said to his puzzled younger brother.

"The captain loves your brother," Itzhak chimed in. "He thinks Abe is one of the finest workers he's ever seen."

"I begged with him to have you taken off the power-line and brought back here to work alongside us. Fortunately, he remembered you, and liked you also. At first he was reluctant, but I persevered. It took some doing, I don't mind telling you, but at last I persuaded him."

"They finally decided to send for you. Oto Mairla told the brass that he had some business to attend to anyway, so he would go to the camp and escort you personally."

"They billeted us all at a place called Coming," added Abe. "They would bring us to the castle every morning to do their dirty work, then take us back at night."

Aron knew of Coming. It was a tiny village about three or four kilometers from the palace.

"The Jews and the barn animals are kept at Coming," Itzhak went on. "They consider us beasts of burden as well, I suppose."

"Sucha has been converted into the local SS base,

64

and the German Army's center for Polish operations. It has become a virtual beehive of activity."

"They keep a hundred of us strong-backed Jews handy to assist them in important matters, shining boots and chopping firewood. After all, winter will be here soon. I tell you, they would be lost without us." Itzhak smiled sarcastically. "Now, it seems, you've become one of those lucky few."

The dark humor of it all wasn't lost on Aron. Jews supplying all of Poland's hard labor while their Nazi overlords relaxed and ran the country.

Aron listened with wonder as his brothers talked. If any of his fondest dreams could possibly come true, then this one surely had. The three of them were back together at last. What was left of the family was now reunited.

Without even speaking of it yet, they all realized that making plans for escape would be their next step.

Among the one hundred workers assigned to Sucha were those with particular talents or trades. Tailors, carpenters, shoemakers, furniture refinishers, and the like, even a few teachers and writers. However, in typical military fashion hardly anyone ever seemed to utilize the skill in which he was adept. Although Aron had been a shoemaker, his most frequent new duties included helping to feed the more than three hundred pigs being raised at the castle.

Abe found himself working inside the mansion, serving at times as a valet and handyman. He would frequently be charged with the responsibility of shining the soldiers' boots, pressing their uniforms, and sometimes delivering their mail. Itzhak, meanwhile, worked mostly in the stable, tending the horses. None of the hundred Jews were ever given steady jobs; and they would often find that switches were made in their regular assignments. If the streets needed cleaning, then they became street cleaners. The loading and unloading of trucks were a part of their chores. Day after day, and month after month. The only pay they received was their food and shelter—and their lives.

The brothers slept in a triple bunk bed, three army cots, one on top of the other. Of all the Jews at Sucha, Abe, perhaps, was the most trusted by the top brass. So much so, that because of his work inside the great house, he was entrusted with a number of keys for various chambers. By chance, he came into possession of a secretly hidden key to the securely locked ammunition room.

The crescent moon hung high in the clear black sky. No lamps were turned on in the workers' barracks. Moonlight beamed inside through the high windows. Unseen, the ever vigilant guards patrolled the perimeters of the village of Coming. Now and then the barking of a German shepherd reminded all of us of the soldiers' constant presence.

Aron leaned over the side of his small bunk. "Any news today, Abe? he asked in a hushed voice. "Have the Russians been able to advance? What about the British? Are they still bombing factories in Germany?"

No one stirred in the barracks as Abe answered, "Nothing to report, yet. But I'll let you know, don't worry."

"Abe, there won't be much time. Steal a few guns, now while you can. Take some ammunition. We're going to need everything we can get."

"Not until the time is right," cautioned Itzhak. "It doesn't matter here if the Soviets have reached Berlin. If the soldiers find that even a single pistol is missing it'll be the end of us."

"He's right," Abe whispered to Aron. "We can't risk

anything now. When we're ready, the day before we're set to run for it, I'll take as many guns and as much ammunition as I can. Count on it."

Aron placed his head on the pillow. His eyes were wide open, staring at the ceiling. Germany was now forced to fight on a number of fronts; against Russia in the East, the allies in the West, and in North Africa, where Rommel was stalled. Rumors circulated that England was planning a new bold strategy, perhaps involving a massive land invasion of Europe. The Italian fascists were tottering. The Americans were landing in England everyday. Convoys were delivering new supplies and weapons.

This was the good news quietly being brooded about. On the other hand, the rumors about the Jews—all of Europe's Jews—were becoming grimmer. More frantic. Nazi Germany was currently embarking upon new and faster solutions to its seemingly never ending problematic 'Jewish Question'. A final outcome that could only result in genocide.

If only they had access to a wireless set, Aron thought. The radio was their only means of communication with the outside world, their only opportunity to learn what was really happening in and beyond the forests of Poland other than the lies promulgated by Nazi propagandists in Berlin.

There were several radios located in the big house, but rarely did Abe have an opportunity to listen and report what he'd heard. The British BBC was regularly broadcasting war news on its short wave bands into most German-occupied territories. America's mighty industry had entered the fight, and brought millions of men under arms. Although the Nazis were hailing victories against all of their enemies, it was quite evident that their war propaganda lacked the ring of

67

truth. The Polish underground organizations were beginning to make some progress in the struggle, and the Germans were intensifying their efforts against them.

The problem was that many of their Polish neighbors were becoming more dangerous for the Jews than the Nazis. Most ruthless of all were the partisans known as the AK, the Home Army For A Free Poland. Claiming that their struggle was for a "clean" Poland free of all enemies, they not only killed German and Ukrainian invaders but Polish Jews as well. This loosely organized 'army' numbered hundreds of thousands in their ranks. It was the largest single partisan organization inside of Poland's borders, mostly armed and funded by the Soviet Union. As far as Aron—and all Jews were concerned—they were little more than opportunistic fascists, no matter on what side they claimed to be fighting.

"When will we attempt our escape, Itzhak?" Aron said at length. "How much longer do we have to wait?"

"Have patience, little brother," replied the sturdy, handsome young man. "We've managed to survive up to now, haven't we? It won't have been for naught. I promise you that. Hold tight, Aron. And pray."

Yes, Aron thought. Indeed he would pray. But at the same time he put his faith not only in God, but also in the authority that a German pistol commands.

Chapter Seven

The Germans came bursting inside the barracks.

"Get up, all of you! Now! *Raus, Raus!*"

It was an all too familiar cry. Dawn had just arrived on this misty morning.

Aron jumped out of his bunk. He exchanged a fearful glance with Itzhak. All along the barrack the bunks were being hurriedly emptied as the young men struggled to their feet, bleary-eyed, shaking off their drowsiness.

"You! You!" the soldiers were shouting. Aron's good friends Meyer Seigleman and Yona Studant were among the first to be taken outside. Behind them marched Philip Borenstein, followed by his brother Nathan. The Borenstein brothers walked straight and tall.

"Move it!"

Aron and Itzhak were jostled down the aisle towards the door. Aron started to protest.

"Be quiet and just do as they say!" whispered the powerfully built Itzhak to his younger brother. They marched gloomily towards the barrack exit.

Abe followed right behind beside another close friend, a youth named Leo Rosenberg. Outside in the gray, chilly morning stood the workers from the opposite barrack, also hastily roused from their sleep, and no less confused. Aron saw the bulky Leibusz Berkowitz brutally knocked down with a rifle butt. Leibusz hadn't moved fast enough. Another youth, Moty Rosenberg, started to help him up but was roughly hustled away by the guards. Leibusz staggered to his feet, his face bloodied, and helplessly faltered behind the rest of the marchers.

"That way!" The soldiers were shouting at them. "Into there, all of you! *Raus!*"

The entire one hundred Jewish workers of Sucha were being herded into a small storage room alongside the barracks. The wooden shed was dark and smelly, reeking of a mixture of aged wet wood, dried animal dung, and spilled kerosene. The heavy, creaking door swung shut and was securely locked.

"What do you think they're planning to do with us?"asked Aron aloud.

Itzhak ran his hand along his stubbled face. Pensively he bit at his lower lip. "Probably just trying to scare us, most likely."

"Maybe they've decided to kill us," offered a shaken Moty Rosenberg. The young man held no illusions when it came to Nazi plans for Jews.

Before Itzhak could join the discussion a voice came screaming through a small hole in the door. It was not a German, but a Pole.

"Hey you, Jews!" he cried loudly, venomously.

70

"They're out there digging holes for you! You Jews are finished!"

They all shuddered.

Abe gasped. "This is the end for us," he muttered bitterly. The incident had left him, and most of the others, badly shaken.

Beside him, another youth dropped to his knees, clasped his hands and started praying in Hebrew.

"Oh, God," called Leo Rosenberg, "he's right. This time we're all done for!"

Frightened, beaten, on the verge of starvation, some of the young people became hysterical. There was no way out of this shed. Nowhere to run. Some banged their fists against the walls, screamed, pleaded to be set free. A few were so scared they were unable to control their body functions.

"Everybody stay calm!" shouted Itzhak above the noise.

He kept his head, and remained calm. It was evident that the sturdy blond youth was one of the camp's most respected leaders. Many followed him, and all respected him.

"Leo, Moty, talk with those fellows over there," he directed. With the help of Aron, Abe, and a friend named Welzu Pojacd, Itzhak did his best to restore order among the group. He could not mitigate the seriousness of their situation. Packed so tightly, in this dark place, there was barely enough room to turn, let alone try to control a frightened crowd.

Aron cursed softly under his breath. He strained to search the walls, the roof, and the door, seeking some weak spot inside of the storage room through which they might somehow break free.

He quickly realized that escape wasn't possible. Not

71

in such confined quarters. Not with armed guards surrounding them on all sides, just itching for the opportunity to open fire. He believed that should someone even try to stick a finger through the tiny hole through which the Pole had shouted, they'd be shot instantly.

"What are we going to do now, Itzhak?"

His older brother wiped beads of sweat from his forehead. "I don't know, Aron—but we're not going to panic. That would be the worst thing that could happen.

Hours passed slowly. At length the weeping and hysteria abated. The pool of workers became morose. Resigned to their fate. Midday and evening passed. It became extremely dark inside.

Aron and his brothers staked out a small place for themselves along one of the room's corners. "Let's try and collect our thoughts," Itzhak suggested as other friends pressed all around, "and try to figure out exactly what is going on."

Abe grimaced. "If they're going to shoot us, then what are they waiting for? Why not do it now and have done with it?"

"Maybe they don't intend to shoot us," said Aron. "Perhaps this is only their way of keeping us fearful."

"If it is," said Itzhak as he pushed a wisp of hair away from his eyes, "then they've succeeded. Look around. The entire camp is hysterical. Whatever the outcome, I think we must realize that Sucha isn't going to end well for any of us."

"Do you have any kind of plan?" asked Yona Studant, who was sitting in the shadows to Itzhak's left.

Itzhak's eyes were cold and calculating. An icy expression marred his handsome features. "I think I'd rather be shot down in the fields than cooped up in a place like this, waiting for them to finish us off. At

72

least, out in the open we might have a chance. We are like confined pigs in a slaughterhouse." He looked around with disgust.

"Death is death," said Mayer Seigleman.

Itzhak glared at him. "Then at least let them kill me in a manner that would allow me to meet my fate with some dignity."

Aron rubbed at his stinging eyes. The air was foul. It reeked from vomit and urine. He turned towards Abe. "If they don't kill us tonight maybe they'll do it tomorrow. Promise me, Abe. If we get out of here alive you'll find those guns for us."

Determination was reflected in Abe's countenance. "The very first chance, Aron. The first chance."

Night passed slowly. A measure of calm overtook the group. The frantic wailing ceased, replaced by an eerie lull.

Some managed to fall into an uneasy sleep, while others, like Aron, kept a constant vigil. Every little sound made his pounding heart almost leap into his throat. Each minute seemed an eternity. Occasionally, he could hear the rumble of a passing truck, and wonder if the vehicle was coming for them. The motors hummed off into the distance. No. Not this one, he told himself every time. Perhaps it will be the next . . .

Now and then he could hear the barking of the prowling guard dogs, or the muffled conversations among the sentries outside and the howling of the frigid wind. Each sound foretokened possible death.

Finally, a new dawn.

Suddenly, the wide door to the storage room banged widely open. A gusty, cold wind blew in.

Aron and Itzhak stood next to one another pensively. The brightness of the daylight made their eyes ache, the force of the wind chilled their bones.

"Out all of you, and back to work!" shouted the soldiers, bearing rifles.

Silently the hundred laborers, grim and anxious, marched onto the muddy grass. Drained and pallid, they loaded themselves onto the waiting trucks that would return them to work at Sucha.

The Germans did not kill any of them—this time.

Several days later four of the hundred youths broke free and made a dash for the woods. A few days later their bodies were found; murdered by the thugs of the AK.

Soon after this incident, SS Captain Oto Mairla sent for Abe. He paced back and forth in his small office at the castle, clasping his hands behind his back. He looked troubled. "Come in," he said in answer to the knock on the door.

"You sent for me?" Abe asked.

Oto Mairla nodded. "The war effort is making new demands on all of us," he informed the worker in his usual detached matter. "Some difficult changes are going to be made here."

It was rumored that the Russians were now giving Nazi Germany a far tougher fight than was anticipated. They were even beginning to turn them back, especially now that America was shipping thousands of tons of weapons to the Bolshevik regime. Once Abe had asked the SS captain how he believed the war would end. "We can handle Russia," Oto Mairla confided, "but with this bear of America to contend with, it won't be easy." That statement had given Abe more hope for survival than anything since the invasion. Perhaps Hitler and his Nazis were not invincible after all.

"The reason I sent for you today," the officer continued, "is that most of the Jews are scheduled to be removed from Sucha. We'll be keeping only fifteen workers at the castle." His gaze met Abe's. "I'd like you to be one of them."

"Where . . . Where are the others being sent?"

Oto Mairla turned his back and stared disconsolately from the window. It seemed to Abe that he was thinking of his distant home and family far away in Munich.

The afternoon light framed his tall figure as he said, "The others are all going to be transferred to Radom."

Radom, a fair-sized city south of Sucha, with a population of a hundred thousand people, had become a smaller version of the Warsaw Ghetto. As many as fifteen to twenty thousand Jews, perhaps more, had been crowded into an area not much larger than the estate itself. If conditions here were deplorable, the Radom Ghetto would be much worse. It was a hell hole of human misery, including starvation, disease, and Nazi brutality; a certain sentence of death.

Abe stood there in stunned silence.

"What do you say, Abe? I can keep you here if you want to stay."

"I would like to stay here, sir." He lowered his gaze as the SS soldier faced him squarely. "But only if my brothers can be allowed to stay also."

With a regretful sigh, the captain said, "I am sorry, Abe. You're a fine young man, and your brothers are good workers, too. But this matter is out of my hands. I can't do anything about it. They'll have to leave."

Abe understood that he could remain relatively safe while under Oto Mairla's watchful supervision. This SS man had always looked out for him. And a transfer to Radom would be worse than a prison sentence. It was a condemnation. Nevertheless, remaining here in safety while his brothers suffered in another city was too onerous a burden for him to bear. If Abe and Aron were to face death, then he would have to join them.

"I want to be with my brothers," he said quietly but firmly.

The soldier sighed, nodding with understanding. "I know how you feel." That was all he said.

So, Abe, too, would be shipped to Radom, as he wished.

The eighty-five refugees from Sucha were again loaded into waiting trucks.

Captain Oto Mairla commanded the journey personally. As the forlorn youths reached the well-guarded gates of Radom, the SS man went to the captain of the police and pointed out Abe in the back of the truck.

"See that boy over there?" he said sternly. "You'd better take good care of him."

It was the last time they saw Captain Oto Mairla.

Aron and his brothers sought out a place in the ghetto to live. They and nine more of the Sucha workers found a single room in the ghetto which they shared; twelve in all. They slept together on the floor. What little food could be found they also shared. Long, arduous days were spent searching for family or friends among the thousands of dispossessed Jews crammed into the ghetto. Neither Abe, Aron, nor Itzhak could find members of their family. Only despair, more fear, and more hunger.

One morning they again were wakened by the shouts of *"Raus!"*

Down in the streets Ukrainians in Nazi uniforms were shooting down anyone who moved. Aron ran outside and hid in a nearby alley. A youth he remembered from his schooldays in Bialobrzegi took

76

refuge in a public toilet. The brawny Ukrainians burst in and shot him. Just another Jew. One less to be concerned with.

The soldiers came marching through the streets firing their guns. It was worse than a pogrom. After they were sated with slaughter, they left.

Wailing women and crying children bent over the bodies of their loved ones. The cobblestoned streets of the Radom ghetto ran red with Jewish blood.

Indeed, comparatively Sucha had been a good life. The mayhem of Radom was a daily nightmare. Many of its soldiers were the scum of the earth. Illiterate and bigoted peasants, mostly brought from distant mountain villages in the Ukraine. Rabidly anti-semitic, most were little more than savages, ready to commit any atrocity as the whim seized them.

Aron was put to work in the fields, cutting blocks of peat, piling them on top of others and leaving them to bake in the sun. He and the others on the labor gang were constantly subjected to abusive screaming, singled out and routinely beaten, for no apparent reason. It was sadism at its worst; more unrelenting than Aron had ever witnessed in Bialobrzegi and Sucha.

Nazi edicts were strictly enforced; the Jews of the city were compelled under duress, to form a special police unit of their own to keep track of the hapless souls in the ghetto. After several months in that abyss called Radom these special police came to Aron, his brothers, and his roommates.

Be ready the next morning, they were told. They were all going to be moved again, taken to another location to work.

"It can't be worse that this hell," Abe remarked.

Aron wondered.

Their newest home was to be Pionki. It was a concentration camp deep within the seemingly endless Polish forests.

Pionki: an ammunitions factory where prisoners produced gunpowder for the German army.

Chapter Eight

Some six hundred new prisoners in a line were marched through half a dozen checkpoints, where they were searched, documented, stripped, and finally inducted into the prison camp in an orderly fashion.

Forced to stand completely naked in front of the guards, they were given blue prison uniforms. Finally, each inmate was assigned to a specific work detail.

Aron was once again detailed to a construction group, mixing and pouring the cement for new buildings for the expansion of the factory's facilities. The Germans wisely assigned Itzhak to the blacksmith shop, where his strong arms were a most appropriate asset. Abe was given the lightest duty of the three: that of gardener.

Barrack number 18 became home for the brothers—a ramshackle building filled with bunk beds and army cots. It was situated directly across the road from the camp's military headquarters.

In all, about twelve thousand men and women worked at the Pionki factory. There were no gas chambers at the concentration camp—but there were frequent executions. Usually by public hanging.

Any prisoners caught trying to excape were brought back, frequently unconscious after severe beatings. The camp officials then would assemble all the prisoners in the large square, where they were forced to gather round the high brick and wood gallows, and compelled to witness the hangings.

Shortly after Aron's arrival, three Jewish boys from the town of Kelc had tried to escape. They were quickly seized and immediately sentenced to die.

Beneath a gray sky it began to shower. The assemblage of prisoners looked on in morose silence. Aron's close friends Aron Tennenbaum and Sam Chaider were among those who watched. Aron was behind them.

As the condemned were led up to the gallows, one of the youths shouted to the crowd, "Brothers! There will come a day!"

The executioner tightened the noose around the condemned man's neck. His eyes were unfocused, his voice frantic.

"Take revenge on the Germans!" he cried in brave but pitiful defiance.

Those were to be his final words; he was trying to shout it again when the little stool was knocked out from under his feet and his body swung wildly in the air.

The other two were quickly executed also.

Aron cringed. The words of the condemned youth remained with him. He repeated them over and over as he passed the lifeless dangling bodies, while walking through the mud on his way to his assigned task.

The desolate, wet corpses remained hanging for days, a cynical reminder to all other prisoners that they could be next.

He shared his fearful thoughts with Sam Chaider. "They're looking for any excuse to finish us off, Sam. One wrong move, a defiant glance, a refusal to obey an order . . ."

"I know it. Be careful, Aron. Guard your every move."

The Pionki prison uniforms were made of a thin, flimsy material that quickly wore out. When that happened, there were no replacements. As the cold, harsh winter weather set in, most of the prisoners sewed rags or whatever they could find over the holes and tears in their tattered clothing.

A girl from Bialobrzegi, no more than sixteen years old, tried to keep warm by fashioning a coat made of burlap and canvas from an old ammunition bag. She kept the garment folded under her uniform so the guards would not see it. One day a German noticed the bulge beneath her uniform and stopped her.

She was terrified as he made her pull out the coat. "Please," she pleaded.

The guard paid no attention to her appeal.

She had to tried to escape, she only attempted to survive the bitter cold. It didn't matter, though.

Feelings of fear and rage simmered within Aron as he watched the soldier take out his pistol and shoot her down where she stood.

She was killed for no reason at all.

Aron quivered with anger and pain. He wanted to wrap his strong hands around the guard's neck, and choke the very life out of this monster. Not to seek justice for the slain child, but out of sheer revenge.

He knew if he did this he too would be dead. He

therefore controlled his fury, looking with hatred at the barbarian in uniform who was a disgrace to the human race. This was cruelty at its vilest.

Again, the words of the boy on the gallows echoed in his mind: *Brothers, there will come a day.* . . .

If he were to have any chance at all of surviving in Pionki he'd have to keep his wits about him. Even in the face of this shocking outrage. Should he dare to even look at the guards in the wrong way, he would be a dead man. When does one day enough? When does a man stand up for justice and dignity? Everything Papa had taught him seemed as fragile as a dream. Words like justice, goodness, kindness, and the rule of law as in the biblical sense. The existing law now was that of the gun. The uncivilized rule of the conquerers over the helpless.

The image of the lifeless girl lying crumpled in the dirt became another picture etched indelibly in his mind.

Because of all these ongoing atrocities he and all the other prisoners lived in perpetual fear, never knowing when their turn would come.

Each day as they went to and from their labors, they marched in line. One hundred prisoners at a time passed through the several checkpoints. The final one was situated directly in front of their barracks.

Aron kept a small crusty piece of bread in his pocket. He'd found a torn fragment of newspaper somewhere and covered the bread with it to keep it clean.

As he passed through the last checkpoint one day, a German sentry examined his pockets. He removed the crumpled newspaper and triumphantly showed the scrap to the chief, a stone-visaged Ukrainian named Janciak. A vindictive man known for his violent hatred of Jews and his sadism.

The Ukrainian grinned with malice as he looked at the piece of old newspaper. "So, you have an interest in politics, eh?" He grabbed Aron by the arm and roughly pulled him to one side.

"Keep the line moving," he growled to his subordinates. "I'll deal with this one myself." Heads bowed, the rest of the work gang passed by in dread silence.

The fragment of paper and the piece of bread had been in Aron's pocket for months. Always previously when it was found it was ignored by the guards. He had never tried to hide it from anyone because he didn't know it would be considered an infraction of the rules. Now, however, this single insignificant item might cost him his life.

Janciak slapped Aron hard on the side of his head, sending him reeling. "You like reading newspapers, do you?"

He screamed so loudly at Aron that the veins in his neck seemed ready to burst. "What are you—a communist? A communist activist?"

Before Aron could attempt a feeble reply the brawny Ukrainian began to beat him mercilessly.

Aron staggered to his knees, then fell to the ground.

From the other side of the gate, in front of the barracks' grounds, Itzhak, Abe, and their cousin, Ester Chaider, watched the cruel proceedings with abject horror.

"God protect him," muttered Itzhak. It was an open secret that anyone who was stopped at a checkpoint had very little chance of remaining alive. It would take a miracle.

For the next hour several German guards savagely pounded the youngster, rendering him unconscious. Each time, however, they revived him with cold water, and continued to beat him.

"They're going to kill him," cried Abe.

In his befogged mind, even as the fists and sticks kept pounding against his flesh, Aron could vividly conjure the image of Papa standing there with him as he was being beaten. And he could hear once again Papa's parting words to him. *Go, my son. Maybe you will survive . . .* The strapping red-bearded man was praying that his son might survive this ordeal.

At length, the soldiers were done with their sadistic pastime. They picked Aron up, dragged him to the checkpoint gate, and pushed him through it. Aron fell in a heap. Bleeding, and on the verge of losing consciousness again, he realized that at least he was still alive. Papa's imagined presence had the effect of easing his pain. His soothing voice was a balm for his suffering.

He collapsed into the arms of his waiting brothers. Itzhak and Abe gently placed Aron down in the grass, beheath the thick boughs of a tree. They washed the blood from his mouth and eyes, and applied a damp cloth over the welts and bruises across his back and ribs where the guards had viciously kicked him with their heavy boots.

"You're going to make it, Aron," the comforting voice of Itzhak whispered soothingly. Aron heard him in a twilight of recognition.

Abe touched Aron's fevered brow. "You're all right, little brother. You're all right. It's over. They won't hurt you anymore."

Aron opened his tumescent eyes with great difficulty. The sight of his caring brothers reassured him, helped him somehow to regain consciousness.

"You're young and strong," Abe was saying. "And you have guts, Aron. You are as brave as anyone I've ever known."

Even in his agony he could see the tears of love they shed for him in their faces. Aron attempted to speak; Itzhak stopped him. "Not now, brother. Not now. Save your strength. In a few days you'll be fine. I promise you."

Even during that lingering moment of despair he was obsessed with the one thing he knew for certain: Even at the risk of his life, he would make his escape from Pionki; from this fascist sewer that robbed men of their self-respect and esteem.

"I'm leaving here," he announced to his brothers about a day later. "What do we have to lose? If we escape, at least there's a chance of surviving on our own. If we stay, we're dead for a certainty." His brothers listened to him without emotion. "If you two want to die, then just stay here and wait for it. I won't."

He sat on the dirt and watched the string of empty wagons roll past the parameters of the camp. They were returning from the trains, the waiting transports that carried his people to the hell known as Treblinka.

Basking in the late afternoon sun, the wagons rolled slowly across the seemingly endless farm fields. Not too long ago these horse drawn vehicles had been used to haul produce, cattle, and horses. Now they were being used to bring his people to the death trains. Jews were pushed from the wagons into the train's cattle cars by the hundreds. Many would die long before they reached their destination. Prior to their deaths some had the courage to scrawl messages on the sides of those wagons and carts. Others were even scribbled on the sides of the train's boxcars. All hoped that these final tragic words would help to save some other life.

With their own blood they wrote. Some in Yiddish, others in Polish.

Don't let them take you. . . .
Run away. . . .
We're going to be gassed—all of us. . . .

These pitiable messages proved conclusively that the worst fears of the Jewish people were indeed tragic realities. That all of them were being gassed and then taken to the hideous crematoriums for the burning of their bodies to ashes, blown in the wind without a trace. This would be the ultimate fate of untold millions of their people if the Nazis had their way.

The terrible crime Jews had committed?

The way they practised their belief in God; itself deserving of capital punishment by the Nazis.

In the shadows of night as Aron anguished and grieved for his people, he recounted what he had seen. His recollections were met with skepticism by his brothers.

"If you won't believe me, then ask our friends who worked with me. They'll tell you what the messages said."

Itzhak searched the still-bruised face of his younger brother. It wasn't that he or Abe believed that Aron was only imagining it—only that what it meant was so grotesque, so unbelievable, it was hard to imagine that any human being could be capable of such debasement of his fellow man.

"All right, Aron," said Itzhak after hearing all the gruesome details. "You've convinced us. And we all know what we have to do."

Abe somberly nodded his agreement. There was nothing left to discuss. The Jewish people were about to be exterminated.

There would no longer be any debate. Their younger brother was right. Definite plans for escape would have to be devised.

Chapter Nine

There were five co-conspirators. Aron, Itzhak and Abe, along with two others, Aron's friend Zisman Birman, and Zisman's friend, Mendl. Zisman Birman came from a village near Radom, called Farle. Mendl hailed from a tiny village called Kfatki, only twelve kilometers from the Pionki factory. He knew the local area well, and was a good contact for them. Once they had breached Pionki's secure parameters Zisman Birman's knowledge of the vicinity would be a valuable asset. His presence among them was particularly welcome.

Unlike the situation at Sucha, here it was impossible for any of them to obtain guns. However, with Itzhak working as a blacksmith they would be able to collect some weapons. Itzhak forged sharp picks and various pointed instruments out of scrap metal. They were deadly weapons, and should anyone stand in their way during their flight, they were prepared to kill if necessary.

It took several long and arduous weeks to become fully prepared and ready to go. Each evening, after their day's labor was completed and their paltry food rations eaten, they would gather under a tree and continue to refine their plans.

What supplies should they take with them? From which of the various checkpoints would it be best to depart? Which direction should they take once they were successfully out and away from Pionki?

Question after question, and each one had to be meticulously discussed and each potential problem satisfactorily resolved. One single error in judgement, or a wrong guess, might forfeit their lives.

The stakes were high.

At length it was decided: Mendl, who was especially well acquainted with the area, would escort the group to a designated point. From there he hoped to find friends and remain with them. Zisman who also knew the local area decided to go with him. The three brothers would then be on their own.

After much discussion Aron, Itzhak, and Abe decided they would search for the rest of their family. While still at the castle at Sucha they heard from another prisoner, that one of their mother's brothers, a man called Meyer Chaider, was hiding with his wife in a place called Biekoska Wola. It was some seventy kilometers from Pionki, a long journey to undertake. It was worth the risk, though, as Itzhak had lived for many years in that village.

After Mama died, Papa, without the means to support all of his seven children, sent Itzhak to live with Mama's father. Their maternal grandfather had been a wealthy man who owned a large farm with orchards and a flour mill on the property. While living with his grandfather, Itzhak had attended school in Biekoska Wola, and had made many friends among the local farmers and tradesmen.

"If we can just make our way to Biekoska Wola," said Itzhak somberly, "We'll be able to survive. I'm sure my friends will be willing to help us."

So they sat beneath the tree, pooling their knowledge, their skills, their ideas on how they should implement them. All that was left was to decide upon the date.

The Pionki labor camp was about fourteen kilometers square. Surrounded by a high barbed wire fence, and constantly patrolled by German sentries and their dogs. The guards were always vigilant, watching everything and every one.

Aron, though, had begun carefully spying on them. He meticulously observed their routine. While they made their rounds at night, he clocked exactly how long it took them to walk from one particular point to another. He committed everything to memory, every movement, and then on each succeeding night he would impart his information to his brothers in minutest detail.

They checked and rechecked, looking for and eliminating any possible flaws. When they were all satisfied, they gave Zisman and Mendl the escape plan, including its point of departure.

Since Zisman and Mendl were quite familiar with the surrounding countryside, they were placed in command of the operation.

Aron sat with them and detailed their strategy.

"Everyday the soldiers march us to and from work along the same road. This route is two kilometers long, passing the lumber yard in which I have been assigned to work. Large trees line both sides of the road, flanked by a ditch. We always cross through the checkpoints in groups of one hundred workers. Soldiers armed with rifles are always watching from both sides, so no one can attempt to slip away."

"Where are we going to make our move?" Zisman, a slender, dark-haired youth of medium height, wanted to know.

"Along the road," Aron answered without hesitation, "as we return from working, heading back towards the barracks."

His preparations were well conceived and thorough. "In between the checkpoints each of us will slip out of our groups, and hide in the ditch. In the dark it will be difficult for anyone to see us. Then, after all the groups have passed, we'll run separately through the ditch and meet at the lumberyard. We'll wait there, and in the period between the changing of the guards, we'll run for it. On our way to freedom." He finished outlining his plan, smiling broadly. It wasn't foolproof; nothing was, but they did have a good possibility of suceeding.

Zisman nodded. "Sounds good to me."

"I think so too," said Mendl.

Itzhak prepared their small arsenal of weapons, several axes, some sharp stakes, and pliers for cutting the barbed wire. He would pass the lumber yard every-day on his way back to the barrack from the blacksmith shop, so Aron placed a heavy stone next to a large tree and each evening Itzhak would toss his newly made weapon next to it. It was Aron's job to retrieve this ordnance and bury it safely away. He buried it all beneath a marked pile of lumber.

Slowly, painstakingly, the group managed to store away some food, as well as a very potent wood alcohol called *ette*, which was used in making gunpowder. One small sip of it could severely burn your insides. That didn't matter. They would drink it anyway. It would prove helpful in fighting the cold.

At last the timing seemed right. When they gathered in the evening and discussed their upcoming work details, it became apparent that each of them would be passing the lumber yard on the next day, which would be a Tuesday.

"Tuesdays are lucky days," one of them had once remarked, repeating an old Polish superstition.

So, 'lucky Tuesday' it was to be.

They would need that luck—and more.

For weeks none of the group had been able to sleep well. They were afraid someone would learn what they were planning. This fear—and the thought of what their punishment would be—kept them all under great tension. Aron felt like a tightrope walker; the smallest misstep would be fatal.

Their cousin, Ester Chaider, was asked if she wanted to join them. She told them honestly that she was too frightened, as were the rest of their friends who were invited to join them.

As the fateful day drew closer, nervousness made it extemely difficult for any of them to hold their food down. Yes, they had planned carefully. But in reality their success depended largely on fate, trust, and luck. They actually had no idea about which way they would have to go, how they would elude any German patrols, or even if they dared show themselves to some innocent Polish farmer.

It was July, 1944. The final Tuesday of the month, seven o'clock at night. The Americans and British had invaded France at Normandy the previous month. Italy had already been lost, Mussolini was deposed by his people a year earlier. The fighting on the Western

Front was fierce as the Allies pressed forward to reach the Rhine. Allied bombings of Germany became more intense, inflicting heavy damage on the Nazi war machine. The Red Army was on the offensive along the Balkans.

Within weeks of the time Aron and his friends planned their escape from Pionki, Adolph Hitler himself had been the target of assassination by a number of his own staff officers who had concealed a bomb in a briefcase during a high command conference. The *Führer* was only slightly injured, however, and continued to defy both military logic and his advisors and pressed on. Especially in the matter of liquidating Europe's Jews. The 'Final Solution' was a priority goal of the Nazis.

These were the events taking place many hundreds of kilometers away when the five prisoners made their own break for freedom.

The sky was foreboding and overcast. Aron was assigned to work in the lumber yard so it wasn't necessary for him to sneak out of line and hide in the ditch. Instead, he hid behind the tall, stacked piles of lumber, and patiently awaited the arrival of the rest of his little group.

It began to drizzle, followed quickly by heavy rain. Thunder boomed across the sky.

He clenched his hands, shut his eyes, and whispered a prayer. "God be with us tonight."

As he peered over the wet wood he saw the first of his friends appear in the distance. A figure sloshing through the mud, followed by another, then the rest. Finally, the five reached the lumberyard. Things had gone as planned.

Itzhak winked at his younger brother. "So far, so good."

They removed their prison uniforms and dressed in the Polish workers' clothes they had gathered; ill-fitting pants, shirts, and caps. Abe wore a beret.

Without a word, Aron led them through the maze of the lumber yard. He had worked there for the previous seven months and had been through every inch of the place. The rain increased in velocity. Aron stopped the group. Holding their breaths, they ducked and waited while a single German sentry passed by the nearby fence. He beamed his flashlight back and forth, grumbling to himself about the weather. When he was gone they dropped on their stomachs and started to crawl. As they reached the fence they stopped, and dug a deep hole leading underneath and out on the other side.

Itzhak wiped mud and rainwater from his face, and cut the barbed wire. The taut wire snapped. Instantly the group scrambled to the other side.

Aron inhaled deeply, and held it. It was his first breath of freedom since the German Army came to Bialobrzegi, and it felt wonderful.

Clutching their weapons tightly, they ran as far and as fast as they could into the night as if they were being chased by demons.

Through the fields and grass they raced, between the trees and over the soggy earth. Helter-skelter, up and down hills, leaping over streams, and stumbling over rocks.

Exhausted, they finally slowed. In the distance, the gloomy lights of Pionki were visible.

Noises reached them from somewhere ahead. Aron held his axe with both hands, ready to spring into action.

A Polish farmer driving an old creaking wagon slowly rolled past.

"You know what will happen if a Pole catches us," cautioned Itzhak.

The question was rhetorical. They all knew only too well. They'd be shot summarily by the Germans or the despised AK thugs. The five young men, however, were strong and tenacious. They would fight back this time, even to the death. Everyone of them had vowed never to return.

"There will probably be a fair number of other farmers around," warned Zisman knowingly. "This entire region abounds in small family farms."

"It doesn't matter," Abe said. "Let's just keep moving."

The continued on, drenched, chilled to their bones, trudging across seemingly endless fields. It wasn't long before Zisman's prediction materialized.

First, a Pole wearing a raincoat, riding a horse. He was soon followed by a farmer driving a wagon. Then others appeared along the scattered grasslands and meadows. Each time a farmer glanced at the group his gaze was greeted with angry, serious faces. It was easy to fathom what was happening. From the way the five moved and acted it was apparent they were on the run.

They also recognized the tenacity and determination in the eyes of these runaways. Words and thoughts that were unspoken by Aron and his friends screamed out loudly at the passing farmers.

Do not try to stop us. Act as though we're not even here. One wrong move on your part and we'll kill you. We're Jews, fugitives, doomed, anyway. So be warned, farmer! We have nothing to lose.

The dismal lights of Pionki at last disappeared from sight. They were well away by now, and probably not yet reported missing at the barracks.

Their mood changed from one of fear to jubilation.

Mendl took the lead, guiding them through the tree filled hills that he knew so well.

It was after ten o'clock at night when the tired and hungry escapees came to a meadow in which was a picturesque farmhouse. The rain had abated a little. "I know this Christian farmer," Mendl told his friends. "He's not a bad fellow. Wait here for me."

He boldly went to the house and knocked on the wooden door.

The farmer opened it and peered perplexedly into the night. A drenched figure in old work clothes greeted him.

"Remember me?" asked Mendl.

The man nodded cautiously. The rest of the group stood in the shadows with their weapons at the ready.

"My friends and I, we need a place to sleep for the night," Mendl went on. "We'd like to dry ourselves too. We have a little money we can give you. Some vodka also."

The farmer led them to the barn, where they slept through the night. In the morning Mendl returned to their host. "Can we stay here with you a few more days?" he asked.

Though he lived in this house alone, having no wife or family, the farmer refused. "You've got to move on," he said. "You can't stay here. If anyone should find out you were here even for this one night, I'll be killed."

Mendl knew that he wasn't lying.

The time for parting had come.

"Zisman and I are going to remain in this area," he told the brothers. "We have reached the place we all agreed upon. You'll have to find your own way from here."

While still working on their escape plans, Aron had

told Itzhak and Abe that if they could reach the power-line, no map would be needed. All they had to do was to follow the line due north. It would lead them home.

Aron knew that this old farmer's house was less than two kilometers from the powerline. Following its trail they would reach the river Pilca, and cross it. The river would then take them to the area of their grandfather's home. There, with any luck, they would find their uncles and cousins in hiding. Although it had been more than a year since any news had been received about the family, the three brothers were confident that they would surely find someone who was still alive.

"God be with you," said Itzhak to Zisman and Mendl.

They all kissed, hugged one another, and cried.

Aron looked deeply into the faces of his friends for what he hoped would not be the last time. "We shall all survive," he said solomnly.

"Yes," agreed Mendl with sadness, "and meet again in better times for us all."

Thus, the last goodbyes were spoken with the two young men with whom they had shared so much, planning, danger, and now the sweet taste of freedom.

It was a difficult and sentimental parting. Aron, Itzhak, and Abe gathered their weapons and trudged up the hill leading away from the little farmhouse.

Dawn had not yet arrived. They stoically walked away, in the direction of the outlying tall columns of the powerline, towards the lovely river Pilca and its shady valleys.

Towards home.

Chapter Ten

The narrow, winding river was there before them. Nestled beside the sandy banks, amid the trees, lived a Christian fisherman with whom Itzhak was acquainted.

Itzhak smiled and was exhilarated at the sign of the little house.

"We've made it," he said triumphantly.

They had traveled a full day, and night, and into the next morning to reach this place. Now, across the beautiful Pilca, snuggled so peacefully in the hills just a few kilometers away, was their destination: Grandfather's village of Biekoska Wola.

"I'm going to go down to speak with the fisherman," Itzhak said. He stretched his aching arms and shoulders, adding, "you'd better hide here in the fields just in case. We don't want any one to see you."

Aron and Abe did as they were told. They watched with a mixture of weariness and joy as Itzhak negotiated his way through the field down to the cottage. It was a warm, beautiful day. A cool breeze wafted over them.

Itzhak disappeared into the cottage to talk with his former neighbor. Fifteen minutes later he emerged, and from his gait Aron suspected that all had not gone well.

Itzhak was distraught and made no effort to hide his tears.

"What happened?" asked Aron.

His oldest brother sobbed. He was barely able to speak. "Dead," he said in a choking voice. "All our friends are dead, killed by the Germans and the Poles."

"And what about Grandfather?" Abe wanted to know.

"They took him away years ago." He shook his head sorrowfully, his shoulders heaving in anguish.

They rested in the field for a while; no one spoke, each was lost in thought. It was difficult for any of them to accept the fact that so many friends they had known all their lives had been slaughtered.

Itzhak managed to clear his head. Putting aside his pain, he said, "Let's get across the river. We're sure to find some living friends on the other side."

Not much of a swimmer, Aron and Abe held Itzhak between them as they forded the twenty-meter wide river. There was another house nearby. It belonged to a kindly Pole they knew named Zajonc.

Zajonc had been mayor of the village, and many years before he'd been a close childhood friend of Mama. He and his wife had always pitied Moshe's family, especially Ester who was forced to assume so many of the family responsibilities after Mama's death. They felt a close kinship with her.

"Such a young girl to have to work so hard, to take care of five brothers and a sister," they would lament with genuine concern.

Aron recalled the couple well. Whenever his family had come to visit with grandfather, Zajonc and his family had been kind and accommodating to them. They would feed the children with as much food as they could eat, and took a special interest in Ester's well being. If only others could have been as caring and charitable as they. Because of their caring, Aron had never forgotten them.

Again, Itzhak approached the house alone, while his brothers took refuge in a corn field. He drew up to his full height and firmly knocked on the door.

The mayor was completely stunned at the sight of Itzhak Goldfarb. He had been certain that all of the family must have perished. After his initial shock, he welcomed Itzhak into his home.

After cordially greeting each other they sat down to talk. "You've changed, Itzhak."

"I'm no longer the boy you remember. Too much has happened. The Germans saw to that."

His host's face grew taut. He had no regard for the Nazis. He scratched his chin, while his grizzled, wrinkled face regarded Itzhak. "What can I do for you?"

"Tell me things I need to know."

"I see." Zajonc lit his pipe as he leaned back and answered Itzhak's pressing questions concerning the whereabouts of Mama's relatives. "For years now I haven't seen or heard from any of your family," he admitted truthfully. "I can't tell you where any of them might be."

"No word from anybody? Not even rumors?"

Sadly, the aging man shook his head. "I'm sorry, my friend. No. Nothing."

Itzhak nodded understandingly. He was deeply disturbed by this news. His mother's childhood friend was well known for his many contacts in the area, and if

Zajonc didn't have any information, it wasn't likely that many others would.

"What are you planning to do? I heard that your brother, Jacob, escaped to Russia."

"He did. Quite a long time ago. Frankly, though, I was looking for your help. . . ."

"My help?" The old man looked quizzically at the strapping youth.

"My brothers and I urgently need a place we can stay for a while," he confided. "Can you find something for us?"

Zajonc leaned forward in his rocking chair. He removed the pipe from his mouth.

"Listen to me, son. If the Germans, or even a neighbor, came here and found any of you, my entire family would suffer. You know what the Nazis do to those found guilty of harboring Jews, don't you?"

"Yes. I know . . ."

"Then please understand, Itzhak," he added with a deep sigh. "I wish I could help, honestly I do, but I can't hide you here."

It was a fact, Itzhak knew. Any Pole, any Christian, who was arrested for harboring Jews would surely pay with his life. Itzhak turned to leave. The mayor stopped him, urging him to at least take some food with him. Itzhak thanked him and carried the package to the corn field. His brothers were waiting anxiously. Once again he told them the bad news.

"What should we do next?" Aron asked while they ate.

Itzhak thought for a time. "There's another fellow whom I know quite well, Czyzak. He's also a farmer, and was a close friend of Grandfather." He considered his brothers, and said seriously. "I think if Czyzak can't find some way to assist us, our situation is going to be hopeless."

They walked the long distance to Czyzak's farm. While Itzhak went to the house the other brothers hid once more. It was already late afternoon. A golden sun was sinking in an almost cloudless sky.

Not long after, Itzhak returned.

"We've got to move away from this place," he said, unnerved. "The earth itself is burning here. Scorched. No one's alive anymore. All the Jews we knew, all of our friends, were killed by the Nazis and Poles, or were sent to the death camps. We have no chance of surviving around here."

This was unexpected and unhappy information indeed. For such a long time they had put their blind hope in reaching this village, certain of finding sanctuary there. They were also sure that some members of their family would be found, and that help would be forthcoming.

Instead they'd come to a desolate place. The village of their grandfather was no longer home. It had become an alien place, and if they did not leave quickly they faced the same fate that befell the others.

Night arrived quickly, the sky suspended like a chandelier of glistening stars. They passed the cottage of a man named Kaczmarek, a young farmer almost as old as Itzhak. For many years his family had worked for their grandfather. Kaczmarek, they unanimously agreed, was not to be trusted. They dared not approach him. His barn, however, seemed enticing, and they really needed a place to sleep. Suffering from total exhaustion, the fatigued and discouraged brothers sneaked into the barn's hayloft.

The fresh hay emitted a pleasant aroma, Aron thought as he rested his head. He fell fast asleep almost immediately. It was Thursday night.

Aron awoke to the sounds of people speaking Polish. He sat up with a start; Itzhak and Abe had already risen, and were intently listening to the conversation.

"They're talking about leaving for church," Abe said, surprised.

"Church?" Aron scratched his head. Hay fell from his hair. "Can it be Sunday?"

It was. They had slept for almost three full days. Fortunately no one had spotted them in the hayloft.

"When everyone returns from mass, I'm going to gamble and have a talk with my old schoolmate, Kaczmarek," said Itzhak, as he brushed himself.

When the farmer returned, Itzhak entered his house. In a few short minutes he came running out. The farmer was frantic as he chased after him and screamed, "Get out! Get the hell out of here!"

Abe and Aron dashed outside. They tried to reason with the angry Kazcmarek. The farmer, however, continued to scream. "You can't stay here! Go away—now! We'll all be killed!"

Once more the three brothers were forced to flee.

Hungry, gasping for breath, they paused well out of sight of the farm. Things were looking quite bleak.

Itzhak leaned against the trunk of a tree. "Maybe there's one last hope," he said pensively. "Another farmer I know, Wozniak, he lives up on the high ground, surrounded by woods. What do you think?"

Aron shrugged. It's worth a try.

Wozniak generously gave them what he could spare; milk, bread, and a packet of cigarettes. Then he, too, sent the brothers on their way, unwilling to risk their presence in his home or on his land.

They left the village with heads bowed. Beside a row of pine trees overlooking the countryside, they rested. Itzhak looked at Aron and Abe tearfully.

"It's a hopeless situation," he said bitterly. "There's no place for us to go. No one will take us in. I'm ashamed of them—all of them. These were my dearest friends." He paused, in distress, adding, "We might as well return to the camp."

"To Pionki?" cried Aron in disbelief.

"Yes."

It was only then that Aron realized that his brother, the strong one of the family, the handsome one, the leader they all looked up to, had been broken by this experience.

"What are you saying?" said an equally startled Abe. He exchanged a furtive glance with his younger brother. "We can't go back now."

Itzhak sat there silently, with his head in his hands and wept. Features sunken and hollow, he finally regained his composure, and said, "Pionki's all we have now. Everything else is gone. Don't either of you see that?"

At last Aron and Abe understood the reasons for their brother's disconsolate mood.

"Poor Itzhak," Aron said softly to Abe. "Coming back here has destroyed him. All the people with whom he had grown up and counted on so much, have all turned him away."

Since fleeing Pionki they'd lived in constant danger, evading not only the Germans, but Polish people as well as the hated AK. They had walked for so long, come so far, passing dozens of villages and towns. As far as they were aware, they were the only three surviving Jews within a radius of perhaps a hundred kilometers.

Along their journeys these recent days it had been Itzhak who buoyed their spirits; he had urged them to keep going, coping with the weather, hunger, and laughing at their weariness as well as their enemies. It was Itzhak who'd been the storyteller, satisfying their hunger not with food, but with fond memories of those he had befriended. "Back home in Grandfather's village my friends will help us find a place to hide," he often said. "I know these people. They are good. You'll see for yourselves when we arrive. Yes, you'll see."

Aron had prayed that his brother would be proven right. That the villagers wouldn't turn their backs on them; Abe similarly hoped to find refuge. Neither, though, counted too heavily on anything more than their own wits. Itzhak had relied on much more. He had put all his trust in those he believed he knew so well.

And now, during this time of his most urgent need, his closest friends had turned him away. He was no longer one of them, as he had been before. They rejected him as if he'd been little more than a stranger.

This painful reality had twisted his insides. Hurt him until their scorn became more painful than any Nazi's punishment. They needed no guns to accomplish this. Only words which could sometimes break more than a man's spirit, and Itzhak had been torn apart. His friends had succeeded where his enemies failed.

The one thing they did learn from this experience, though—in this area the Nazis and Poles were working in collusion with one another—every farmer and villager was a potential enemy. They could rely on no one.

"At least we had food at Pionki," Itzhak reminded them. There was a tone of dejection in his voice. "We had a place to rest our heads. Here nobody wants us. Nobody."

Aron listened and tried to comfort him, knowing this wasn't really his brother saying these things, only a broken man. It was tragic to witness.

"Maybe if we sneak back into the camp the Germans won't notice that we ever left," Itzhak added.

Aron wiped tears from his eyes. It broke his heart to see what had become of his beloved brother.

"Itzhak," he said, "you've been schooled in crop management. Abe is a fine tailor. I can make shoes. Certainly with our combined skills we should be able to get along somehow. Hide somewhere—"

"Where?"

"The forest, a cave, anywhere. What does it matter? We must live. We have to *survive*!"

Itzhak's gaze was blank.

It seemed that everything had fallen apart. All their plans and their dreams. They had fought tenaciously, clawed and struggled to reach this awful place, only to be turned away at every door. Had their escape been for naught?

Abe quietly tried to convince Itzhak that returning to the camp would be a serious mistake. Itzhak wouldn't listen. He remained adamant.

There was nowhere else for them to go, he insisted, no place for them to hide. No one wanted them. Their entire world consisted only of a dot on a map, known as Poland. It was the only home they knew, and they were now convinced that it would be the only one they would ever know.

"We've been gone barely a week," said Abe. "Don't we owe it to ourselves to try to buy a bit more time? We haven't needed anyone's help so far. We can make it on our own without any of these people."

Again Itzhak rejected the argument. "I say, we return."

Abe held his ground. "I vote that we stay." He turned towards Aron. "We are evenly divided; you break the tie, Aron, decide."

Aron considered the pros and cons. Itzhak of course was right about one thing: no matter where they went, everything seemed to be against them. The Germans, the AK, the Poles, and now even their lifelong friends had abandoned them. In the hell that was Pionki, they had at least been among their own people. Friends who would stand beside them.

Throughout the long years of pogroms, persecutions against the Jews, Papa had refused to emigrate from Poland with his family. He had thrown in his lot with his fellow Jews in their country. Perhaps now they should also do likewise, remain among their own, and whatever fate has in store for the Jews in Pionki, let it be theirs as well. Aron was sure that this would have been Papa's wish.

Aron was exhausted by this ordeal. He was also on the verge of giving up. His disappointment was keener than he was willing to admit. Maybe Itzhak's way would be better, who could say? Their perilous freedom had been a bitter pill to swallow indeed. It had crushed Itzhak.

"Vote, Aron," said Itzhak at last.

He looked into the aggrieved eyes of his oldest brother, placed his hand on his shoulder, "all right," he said. "I'll stay with you, Itzhak. I'll return to Pionki."

Abe was strongly opposed to this rash decision. Nevertheless, he reluctantly agreed to return also, feeling that as brothers they were obligated to remain together.

To the eyes of the occupying Germans, the brothers looked no different from anyone else in the Polish countryside. To the Polish people, however, they could be easily identified as Jews. Aron knew, quite well, that a free man's mien was different from that of a prisoner; fright is reflected in one's behavior. Thus, when a Pole met them, they could recognize them as runaway Jews.

The trek back to Pionki would be a difficult ordeal for them. They would not only be trying to avoid Germans but Poles as well.

They crossed the river again, this time without hope or enthusiasm. It was decided that before entering Pionki proper they would stop at the home of the farmer who had given them refuge that first night of freedom, near the village of Kfatki.

In Kfatki lived a Polish woman who worked as a specialist in the Pionki factory. Her name was Maria. She was not a Jew, nor a prisoner, but hired by the Germans to work for them.

Maria had little love for Nazis and she, it was hoped, could provide them with valuable information. Above all, they needed to know if the Jews were still stationed at the camp. After being isolated in the woods for some time, it was possible that the prisoners were no longer there, perhaps already taken to the death trains. There might possibly be no place to return to at all.

The eighty-kilometer journey back proved to be far more taxing than the one they had first undertaken that night from the lumberyard. There was no longer any hope in their hearts. No joviality. And a loss of faith in the brotherhood of man. They were what they were: a trio of escaped Jews. Homeless, dispirited, and bereft of hopeful expectations.

The hours dragged as they walked endlessly, through valleys, over fields, through wild grass, among the tall trees and the seemingly endless forests of Poland.

After walking all night they came at last to the tiny cottage where they had first found refuge. Itzhak asked if the farmer would hide them for a day or two.

He refused at first, citing the dangers. Then, when he was offered the few coins the brothers still had, he agreed to let them stay for one day.

Aron slept soundly. His courage was deserting him, and like Itzhak he was now willing to share the fate of the Jewish prisoners.

Late during the following night, the brothers walked together through the field, discussing their next move. The moon was bright above the distant tree line.

"Look over there," said Abe, gesturing beyond the high grass. A silhouette darted low against the ground.

The brothers instantly dropped to their knees. Aron signaled for Abe and Itzhak to spread out, move carefully toward the unknown intruder. He felt his pulse quicken. It wasn't a German soldier, he was sure.

Then who? An armed partisan seeking refuge? AK saboteurs? He was prepared for anything.

Suddenly, he heard a familiar sound; a clicking noise, rapid and low. He raised his brows in surprise. It was the same signal he and his fellow escapees had used as a code among themselves.

With quickened heartbeats, Aron repeated the clicking sound in reply.

The silhouette stood upright. He was bathed in moonlight.

It was Zisman Birman.

"Zisman," cried Itzhak, recognizing him instantly. He sheathed his knife.

Zisman ecstatically ran and threw his arms around his compatriots. "My God, I never dreamed I'd ever see any of you again."

"Zisman, what in heaven's name are you doing here?" asked Aron, as he put away his own weapon. "By this time we thought you were well hidden."

His friend pushed back his worker's hat, and shook his head sadly. "Mendl took off by himself a few days ago, while I was asleep. I don't know why or what's happened to him." Zisman ran his forearm across his mouth. "Ever since then I've just been wandering aimlessly through these fields with no destination, like a lost man." He gazed at the brothers individually. "What are you three doing back here? I thought, by this time you'd be well across the Pilca river and in your own territory . . ."

"We were," said Itzhak grimly.

He proceeded briefly to describe their unhappy adventure and the bitter conclusions they were forced to accept.

"I'm not surprised," said Zisman with a scowl. "I doubt if there is anyone who can be trusted these days. Jews can only depend on each other."

Sadly, his own travels had resulted in similar disappointments; old friends who turned their backs on him repeatedly.

"We have therefore decided to return to Pionki."

Zisman fully understood. "Freedom wasn't what any of us thought it would be, was it?"

"We're on our way to Kfatki, to speak with Maria," said Aron. "If she gives us her approval we'll slip back into camp. Will you be returning with us?"

"I will," Zisman answered looking quite serious. His father and younger sister were still prisoners at the camp. He was greatly concerned for them.

"Alright, so it seems that we're together again," cried Itzhak. He embraced his old accomplice tightly and grinned.

It was good to see his oldest brother exhibit even a hint of cheerfulness again, Aron knew. It was their good fortune to find Zisman tonight, and in him they surely had a true friend. One who would stand by them through all adversity.

"Then what are we waiting for?"

Abe shrugged. "Let's go."

Chapter Eleven

It was decided that it would be too dangerous for all four of them to make the five-kilometer trip to Kfatki together. Among all the other dangers, they knew that the German eastward armies were engaged in furious battles with approaching front line Russian units. With this Red Army advance, the Eastern Front was rapidly approaching. The Wehrmacht was cracking. But it would be a long time before it broke.

"I'll volunteer to go into the village," said Aron.

"No, I'll do it by myself," Itzhak volunteered.

Of the three brothers he was the least likely to be caught. Not only was he the tallest and strongest of the group, but his command of the Polish language was excellent. More than anyone else, he'd be able to mingle among the Poles and pass as one of them.

"It would be better if I came along with you," offered Zisman. He was also fluent in the local dialect, and an expert in the logistics of this territory.

"All right," agreed Itzhak. "Just the two of us." He turned to his brothers. "I want you to hide in the farmer's hayloft. He's sure that we all left some time ago, and won't be checking on us."

"How long are we supposed to wait?" Aron wanted to know.

Itzhak looked up into the early morning sun. He judged the time to be about eight o'clock. "With any luck we'll locate the house of this woman, Maria, and be back here at, oh, maybe around noon time."

"But if we are delayed for any reason," added Zisman, "stay where you are. Sooner or later we'll join you."

"Got that?"

Aron and Abe nodded. Itzhak smiled. "See you later."

It was warm and breezy that morning as they set off for Kfatki. Aron and Abe both waved, then walked off towards the barn. They took refuge high in the straw-covered hayloft. There they waited impatiently.

A little while later a number of blackbirds crossed the sky above the field where Itzhak and Zisman had walked. Then they flew through the open doors of the barn.

The sight of them made Aron shiver. Blackbirds were considered to be an ill omen among the peasants of Poland, and that thought troubled him. Trying not to take the ancient superstition too seriously, he became overwhelmed by a sudden feeling of dread and impending doom.

Stop this nonsense, he said to himself.

But a nagging voice inside of him warned that something was amiss, and persisted. Aron kept quiet, and said nothing about the incident to Abe.

However, Abe had also noticed the birds, and as

111

Aron did, he did not mention the old wives' tale. Neither wanted to frighten the other.

Time passed slowly. No one came or went. The afternoon sun began to sink in the horizon. Aron squinted and searched the empty fields. There was still no sight of either his brother or his companion. He was getting very worried.

Night fell. A cool, pleasant wind rustled through the tree branches and grassy fields. Aron could not fall asleep, and neither could Abe. All that night they kept a constant vigil.

Dawn came, and they still waited. Birds were chirping in the trees. It was a beautiful morning, the grass glistening in golden sunlight.

Zisman had told them to remain where they were, and continue to wait. Another long day passed. Aron prayed for their safety. The appearance of the blackbirds bothered him more than ever.

"What do you think we should do?" asked Abe as another night passed.

"Give them a little more time. Many things might have delayed them . . ."

The faraway boom of heavy guns echoed like thunder.

A battle was raging fiercely along the front with the German artillery clashing with the Russian. They could hear the whistle of bombarding shells, see the night sky ablaze as mortar rounds blasted their distant targets repeatedly without any abatement. Each side suffered punishing blows.

Perhaps Itzhak and Zisman were hiding from German troops along the road. Nazi convoys were constantly racing to the front. Perhaps they were unable to leave the village of Kfatki because of the close proximity of the fighting. They might even have been caught in a crossfire, pinned down until the battle was over.

Anything was possible.

That's what Aron was hoping.

On the previous morning Itzhak and Zisman had crossed the field and followed the winding road to the village. Workers' caps pulled low over their foreheads, jackets concealing their knives, they made no effort to hide from anyone. Rather, they hoped to successfully pose as local peasants making their way to the village.

It was getting warmer. Zisman stopped to drink from a stream. "When we get there let me be the one to ask where to find her house," he said. "I know the village. If anyone questions us I'll tell them I'm her nephew or something like that."

Itzhak checked to see if his knife was well secured in his belt. "All right, but don't be too eager to answer questions. We don't want to become the center of attention."

Zisman wiped his mouth. He gazed off into the distance. "We should be there in a few minutes," he said, gesturing along the downward slope of the next hill. Kfatki was nestled right behind it.

A farmer on the buckboard of a wagon paid no attention as the two strangers clad in workers' clothes crossed his path.

"My feet ache," Zisman muttered. He picked small stones from the soles of his worn shoes. The walk from the farm had taken about two hours.

There were gardens in the front or the rear of all of the picturesque cottages along the dusty road. Flowers were in full bloom, and Itzhak inhaled their pleasant fragrance. He loved flowers. A cluster of quaint village houses lay before them.

"Let's hope we can get in and out of here as fast as possible," Itzhak said.

"You don't have to remind me."

A dog barked as they continued to walk. Noises emanated from a chicken coop where feed had been spread over a patch of spotty dry grass.

Several grizzled, stocky men in shirt-sleeves had gathered near a well from which housewives were carrying buckets of water. Tethered horses were drinking from a trough. The men stood around mumbling among themselves while they watered their horses. One was holding an almost empty bottle of vodka. They started to laugh over some joke when they caught sight of the two approaching strangers.

"I think they're partisans!" whispered Zisman.

"Don't even acknowledge their stares," cautioned Itzhak. "Just pretend we're going about our business."

"There's an old fellow in a rocking chair on that porch," said Zisman, pointing to a pleasant stone house across the road. "He's lived here all his life. I'm going to ask him where Maria's house is."

"All right, just be careful."

Zisman sauntered towards the whitewashed cottage as if he hadn't a care in the world. Great trees lined both sides. He could hear a pig snorting in the backyard.

"Excuse me," he called out to the farmer.

Someone shouted at them from behind. Both young men turned. It was one of the weather-beaten men in shirt-sleeves. A large broad-shouldered man with light hair and piercing blue eyes. Two of his companions stood closely behind him.

"Were you shouting to us?" said Itzhak, affecting his finest Polish.

The shirt-sleeved man nodded. He cocked his head slightly, looked at them with distrustful eyes, and placed his hands to his hips. He was wearing a gun belt. A fourth partisan soon joined the group. This younger one was wearing a long jacket with a heavy bulge under it. He was probably carrying a rifle.

"Is there a problem?" asked Zisman, trying not to appear nervous.

"No, no problem." The shirt-sleeved man moved several steps closer. "Where do you two come from?" he inquired in a husky voice.

"South. A village near Radom."

"And what are you doing here?"

"I have an aunt in Kfatki. Maria—" He paused as several more men emerged from a barnlike structure and moved closer to them. "I came to see her."

"And your friend?" Their eyes focused on Itzhak.

"We work together."

"These are dangerous times," said the partisan, his gaze fastened on Itzhak. "These hills are full of Poland's enemies."

"We know. We saw a number of German convoys. They were moving east. Towards the front."

Some of the men nodded knowingly. Convoys had recently passed this area. "What do you have with you? Any money?"

"Not very much. Only a few *slotas* among us."

"What about cigarettes?"

Both Itzhak and Zisman shook their heads.

"Your clothes are filthy," another said. You're dressed in city attire. It looks like you've been wearing them for weeks."

"The Germans held us up for questioning a few days ago. They kept us in detention."

115

"So they let you go?"

"After a few days, yes," Itzhak said boldly. "They had no reason to detain us."

"Do you have your papers?" The shirt-sleeved partisan held out his hand.

Zisman stood his ground. "Why do you want our papers? Are you the police?"

"We only want to know who you are."

"Who are *you?*"

Proudly, he said, "members of the Polish underground. Fighters for a free Poland. And Kfatki has been placed under our protection now."

AK, Itzhak realized. To him they were the scum of the earth. A loosely-knit brotherhood of hoodlums and criminals who referred to themselves as patriots.

"Do you think we're spies?" Itzhak asked. "You think we're Germans in disguise?"

One of the jacketed men brandished his German rifle. A spoil of war taken from a corpse. "We've been scouring the hills of this area for weeks. Routing all our enemies. SS, Ukrainians, Jews, even some Russians." He spat on the ground.

"I see you ran into some German patriots," said Itzhak, eyeing the gun.

The rifleman fondled his weapon. "A German patrol ran into *us,*" he corrected. They all chuckled as he continued, "along with some of their Ukrainian mongrels."

A long butcher's knife glinted from the waist of another. "They didn't give us much of a fight, though."

"Good," said Zisman. "It's time we rid Poland of all its foreign invaders."

"Including Jews." It was the shirt-sleeved man who spoke. He held out his hand. "So show us your papers —Right now!"

Itzhak and Zisman shared a quick glance. These men did not belong to the organized Polish resistance. As members of the detested AK, they were ruthless, pillaging outlaws and murderers, intent on creating from the ashes of Poland, a fascist-free Poland, which they would rule.

From out of the corner of his eye Itzhak counted six men, all hardened and armed. The odds were worsening.

"I have our papers," bluffed Zisman.

He pretended to search in his pockets, stalling for even a moment. One of the thugs removed a German lugar from its holster. There was no doubt that he intended to use it.

Itzhak quickly glanced at the surroundings. Opposite the farmhouse was a sloping field of fairly high grazing grass surrounded by low fences. Their only possible escape route was across that field, and they didn't have much time.

"Run!" shouted Itzhak.

The two youths dashed for the open field along the road.

"After them—they're Jews!" shouted the man brandishing his pistol.

Shots rang out. Zisman tumbled and fell.

Itzhak raced through the deep grass and crawled on his belly. Nearby, Zisman lay bleeding, his leg shattered. He tried to inch his way across the grass in a fruitless effort to elude his attackers.

Itzhak looked on in horror as two AK men stood over the wriggling figure and pumped bullets into him. Zisman screamed. His body quivered, momentarily twitched, then finally was motionless.

"Quick, find the other one!"

Knife in hand, Itzhak crept through the deep grass.

Beyond the field lay a wide gully containing huge boulders. If he could get there, he might be able to hide or run for the cover provided by the trees.

"I see him! Over there!"

A rifle shot rang out. The bullet screeched beside Itzhak, and sent dirt flying only a meter away. The armed AK men fanned out over the grass. Itzhak's eyes measured the distance to the gully. With one quick move he rose, lowered his head and shoulders and bounded towards safety.

Gunfire cracked.

He felt a sudden, hot flash down his spine. Itzhak staggered and fell. Blood stained the grass. Flat on his back, his eyes wide, he clasped his knife. A thin stream of blood flowed from the side of his mouth.

This was the end, he realized. But if he could kill only one of his sworn enemies, he thought, perhaps his death would not be in vain. Just one. . . .

"Let the Jew bleed to death," someone said.

"No. I want to watch him die."

A figure loomed over him. The pistol pointed straight at his heart. Itzhak tried to hide his fear. Painfully he gritted his teeth.

A crow squawked as the sound of the bullet echoed through the lonely field.

For Itzhak it was all over.

The murderer put his gun away and lit a cigarette. "Two less Jews," was all he said.

Part Three

Chapter Twelve

At midnight Aron and Abe decided to leave the safety of the hayloft. They washed in a nearby stream. As clouds passed across the moon, Aron saw what looked like a man lurking in the bushes. The barrage of gunfire from the east shook the ground like an earthquake. Aron drew his knife and waited breathlessly.

The stranger approached the stream slowly, watching Abe and himself as searchingly as the two brothers followed his movements.

"Amchu!" a voice called out. It was a Yiddish word, meaning, 'I'm one of you,'; a phrase frequently used among the Jews, and one a Christian would be unlikely to understand.

Aron and Abe sheathed their knives.

Dressed in a long, worn raincoat, wearing a tattered cap, their visitor openly presented himself.

"Who are you?" said Abe uneasily.

"I'm called David," the man replied. "I'm a Jew, the

121

same as you." He was bedraggled and unkempt, with long, matted hair trailing down his forehead and over his ears, torn shoes and pants. He looked more like a derelict or beggar than a fugitive and tucked under his arm was a weapon; a sawed-off shotgun.

"What are you doing here?" asked Aron. He and Abe glanced at each other dubiously.

David kneeled to drink water from the stream. The heavy artillery and mortar bombardment continued unnervingly in the background. "I come this way sometimes," he answered, wiping his mouth on his sleeve. "I've been hiding in these woods for the last three years." He patted his shotgun. "Alone, except for my comrade here."

"For three years?"

David nodded dourly. "I sleep out in the open, under the trees. Steal food when I can, or shoot it. I meet no one, and trust no one." From the way he spoke and acted he seemed to be an eccentric character without all of his wits about him.

"What brings you here?" asked David.

Reluctantly the brothers told him their story of escape from Pionki, and how and why they decided to return.

"Now," Aron went on, "we have been waiting for our brother and another friend who went down into the village."

David regarded them with baleful eyes. "Brothers," he said, "you don't have to wait any longer. His voice was hushed, his face twisted with regret. "The AK killed your brother and friend yesterday morning."

Abe grew angry; his voice rose above the boom of shell fire. "How do you know any of this?" he demanded.

122

David put his hands out, palms open, in a peaceful gesture. "I'm sorry to have to be the one to bring you this sad news. I still have a few Christian contacts in this area. They told me that two Jewish young men were murdered in Kfatki yesterday, just as the AK had killed another Jew called Mendl, a few days earlier."

Aron and Abe sat beside the stream in total disbelief. They listened as David continued relating everything he'd been told, crying as he talked. David told them how the detested AK had been hunting him also, and how he'd managed to narrowly escape. Everything he said made sense, they knew, but the brothers still had some reservations about trusting this unusual stranger. They wanted more evidence and corroboration.

"What are you two going to do now?" asked David.

Aron shrugged, avoiding the question. "We'll move on somewhere."

"You can travel with me, brothers. I would enjoy having companions."

His offer surprised them. "You want us to accompany you?"

"I have this gun, and some ammunition. I know this whole area like the back of my hand." He gestured around him into the night. "I'll take you to places deep in the woods where we'll never be found. . . ."

Shaking his head, Abe said, "Thank you, but no. We can't. We won't be staying around here very much longer. Better for us if we try to find a hiding place in some area with which we are more familiar."

"Are you sure? We can keep each other company, watch out for each other . . ."

Again the brothers refused the offer.

"Our heartfelt thanks to you, David, for letting us

123

know what happened. We'll never forget. God be with you."

David nodded. He stood up squarely, hefted his shotgun back under his arm. "I'm sorry, then. May your brother and friend find peace at last. And may God be with you, too."

With that he turned and disappeared back into the night, as mysteriously as he first appeared. Aron and Abe walked off in another direction. When they were certain that David was well away, they sneaked back into the farmer's barn.

They slept restlessly until dawn.

"What do you think?" said Aron, after they awoke.

"I think he was telling the truth," answered Abe. "But we still had to be sure."

Aron agreed. They could not let the news of Itzhak's death depend solely upon the word of an odd-ball wanderer. Who knew what tortures and horrors David had witnessed or experienced. His mind might have become irrational. Perhaps he confused Itzhak and Zisman with some other poor souls.

"I have an idea," said Aron. He reached into his pockets and took out whatever money he had. "Let's ask the farmer to go into Kfatki and ask around for us. We'll pay him. He's well known to the villagers and they won't suspect him."

The farmer took their money and agreed to their request. He left in the morning and returned in the afternoon. The brothers were anxiously waiting.

"I'm sorry to tell you this, but what you were told is true," reported the farmer. "The AK, *Armia Krajowa*, killed two Jewish strangers in Kfatki a couple of days ago. Your brother Itzhak is dead, as is your friend Zisman."

Tears streamed down their faces as they stood helpless before the farmer.

"Why don't you leave?" said the farmer without emotion. "There's nothing left for you here anymore."

They told him that they would go. But at night, they once again returned to the barn, hoping to get some sleep before the early morning hours before leaving.

It was almost midnight when Abe woke with a start from the yelling and pounding at the farmer's house. He peered out from the loft. Heavily armed men with flashlights were shouting.

"Some Jews are hiding here! Where are they?" They began to beat the farmer.

"Get up, Aron!" Abe whispered urgently. "It's the AK!"

Aron rose groggily from a deep sleep. Abe yanked him by his hair. "What—?"

"*Shhh.* Listen. They've found us."

The farmer, on his knees, face bloodied, pleaded with his assailants. "There are no Jews here," he wept. "I swear it. I swear it."

The thugs paid no attention; they continued to beat the man mercilessly.

Abe quickly covered his sleepy brother with hay, slipped down from the hayloft and ran out into the corn field.

Lying on the floor, covered with straw, Aron finally came to his senses. The beams of flashlights came through the wooden slats of the barn as he retreated breathlessly into the dark recesses of the hayloft. There he lay perfectly still, too terrified to move. Several of the AK partisans entered the barn. They looked around, scanning the beams of their flashlights in several directions. Aron felt his thumping heart pound against his chest. He held his breath while the bandits climbed up to the hayloft and poked into various clumps of hay.

Aron knew that if he made the slightest movement

125

they would find and kill him instantly. Sweat poured down his face. He clenched his teeth tightly and tried not to scream in fear.

"There's no one in here," one of them finally reported.

A moment later they descended and went back outside.

"Where are the Jews hiding?" they insistently demanded of the helpless farmer. He shook his head, crying. They resumed beating him until they tired of it. At length they left.

Aron made his way down from the hayloft. He raced through the darkness and out into the corn field. Abe saw him and signaled.

"Let's get away from here as fast as we can," he said.

They walked into the July night with no idea where they were heading. Their only objective was to evade the AK again and find some other shelter.

Hours passed. They crossed fields and meadows, climbed over rugged, rocky hills, then back down again. They passed another village. Exhausted, they searched for some place to rest.

Along the road they spotted a a barn with a ladder propped against the wall on the outside, leading to the hayloft. Though they had no idea who the owner of this land might be, they decided to take the risk. They climbed up into the hayloft, and pulled the ladder up behind them.

As they rested, they once again heard shouting. They were aghast as they looked outside, realizing that the same AK gangsters had come here too.

The brother strained to listen to the distant conversation. They couldn't overhear much, only enough to learn that this farmer was a shoemaker or had one working for him. From the way it sounded it seemed that the AK men were waking him because they wanted someone to repair their boots. They were not searching for escaped Jews after all, as it turned out. They began to brutally beat this farmer also. He moaned as they knocked him down and pounded him repeatedly until he, too, lay bloodied and groaning. No 'crime' had been involved. His only mistake had apparently been his refusal to repair their boots in the middle of the night.

When they left, Aron and Abe scrambled down from the loft and ran. This area was a far too dangerous one in which to remain, they realized. No one was safe from these partisan "freedom fighters"—not even their fellow Poles.

It was still dark. Tired as they were, they kept walking. Endlessly walking.

Aron's worries were compounded. What would be their next step? Where might they go from here?

"We'll return to the castle," Abe told his weary younger brother. "Back to Sucha."

When they were sent to Radom, Abe's job at the great estate had been taken by a Pole named Janek Koptera. "This Koptera is a good man," Abe said to Aron. Then as he recalled Itzhak's disappointments and anguish, he quickly added, "At least I believe he is. We'll chance it and stop at his house. Maybe this time we'll find help."

Chapter Thirteen

Once again they devised a plan, a direction to take, a destination to reach. At last there was a glimmer of new found hope. They followed the sprawling power-line to Radom. Farms and fields, warm under the summer sun, dotted the landscape.

Occasionally they ran into local Polish villagers and farmers. Not recognized as Jews, they explained how they had just escaped from interrogation by the Germans. They made the sign of the cross when they spoke of their trials and tribulations, and those listening empathized with their suffering countrymen. Food was readily offered, and sometimes a place to rest or sleep. On and on they walked, all through the hot day and the cool night.

It was early evening when they reached the familiar Sucha. Lamplight glowed from inside Koptera's small cottage. Less than two hundred meters along the road, was the SS headquarters.

The brothers paused, hiding among the leafy trees. Here they would be recognized; all the local citizenry knew Aron and Abe. They couldn't risk being seen by anyone.

Aron waited nervously outside, smoking a cigarette while Abe found a way to sneak into Koptera's house. After a short while Koptera came out to speak with Aron.

"It's too dangerous for us to talk here," he said. He pointed towards the multi-domed palace in the distance. "There's an attic above the ice cellar. It'll be a good place to talk."

The ice cellar was a cooled, storage room built below ground where the Germans stored all their perishable foods. It was one of Koptera's numerous duties at Sucha to bring food up from the cellar to the kitchen where cooks prepared meals for the SS officers.

"I remember the place," said Aron.

The Gestapo, in fact, ate quite well indeed. No shortages of anything for them. But the so-called attic was hardly a room at all, merely an empty space atop the storage cellar, and directly beneath the ground level. Anyone could, and often did, walk right over it.

Koptera, a stocky man with a thick moustache, continued by saying, "I know how tired you must be after such a long journey. At least you'll be able to rest up in there."

Aron looked at him distrustfully. It was not unexpected, Koptera was well aware of the reasons.

"Don't be afraid," he said. "I'm not going to turn you in. Just stay in the attic and wait for me. The next time the Germans send me down to the cellar for food, I'll sneak some out for you and your brother. You won't starve."

The brothers looked at each other. Then they agreed to the plan. They had nothing to lose.

Following Koptera's advice, they managed to get down into the cellar, crawling carefully to the small attic shelter. They found that it was little more than a crawlspace, with a very low ceiling. Its 'floor' was covered with thick layers of sawdust, which would make it too itchy for them to lie on. The air inside was stifling and dank. If they were considering it as a place to rest they would need a covering for the sawdust.

"Straw mats will do fine," said Abe. "I know just the place to find them—the greenhouse."

As Abe crept closer to the guarded greenhouse a bright light flashed in his eyes. His heart skipped a beat.

"They've found me!" he thought, surely an SS man with flashlight would be staring down at him. He waited to be caught and ordered to stand. However, nothing happened.

It was not a soldier with a flashlight. It was only a reflection of the moon, shining brightly and reflecting on the greenhouse glass. Abe breathed a deep sigh of relief. Carefully, he entered. First he picked up a couple of mats, then a few tomatoes and other vegetables. Arms filled, he raced in the shadows back to the attic.

They lay down on the mats. Their experience had been precarious and more taxing than they realized. As he rested, Aron estimated that they had walked a distance of almost 300 kilometers, from Pionki to their grandfather's village, then back again towards the camp, and now to Sucha. They were close, once more, to Bialobrzegi, the town they once called home. Quite ironic, though, was the fact that only fifty meters from their new, safe haven was SS headquarters, the very embodiment of the Nazi authority from which they were fleeing. The irony of the situation was not lost on the brothers.

It soon became difficult for Aron to keep his eyes open. As he recalled the perilous journey, the pointless deaths of Itzhak and so many of their friends, he fell into a long, deep sleep. It took three days for the brothers to recover from their shared ordeal.

True to his promise, Koptera brought them as much food as he could safely steal. For the first time in many months the two were able to relax. They converted the attic into a sort of small home for themselves. A place where they could continue to hide, while they prayed for the war to end quickly.

This was the kind of hiding place that Abe had all along wanted for the brothers to hide. During the years he worked at Sucha he familiarized himself with virtually every centimeter of the estate and its vast grounds. He knew its building, the layout, the nearby fields, the surrounding forests, and even the comings and goings of the soldiers stationed there.

Of course they realized the risks they were taking. This was a dangerous hiding place indeed. A refuge under the very noses of the Germans. When they first arrived at Sucha the palace housed perhaps fifty soldiers. Within a few weeks, however, the estate accommodated hundreds of members of the German military—all of whom, at one time or another, walked by the ice cellar.

And now, the number of troops stationed there had multiplied like rabbits. Convoys were rolling in and out of Sucha's grounds, constantly shuttling back and forth from the ever-narrowing Eastern Front and the advancing Red Army.

Despite all of these dangers, Aron and his brother

131

were able to live an ordinary albeit vulnerable day-by-day life, until something quite unexpected threatened their safety.

From the tiny hatch that opened onto ground level they commanded a broad view of the road leading to and from the castle. One morning an SS officer named Petzolt, second-in-command of the fortress, came strolling by with a huge German shepherd dog at his side. The animal, unleashed, suddenly began to bark. He sniffed and walked towards the wooden covering of the ice cellar. There he began to scratch with his big paws, and stuck in nose into a small hole.

Abe drew back in disbelief. The dog remained there for a time, right above the two huddled, frightened brothers.

Petzolt yelled at the dog, who raised his head and looked back at the soldier, then at the dirt above the ice cellar. After another call, the dog returned to the waiting soldier, and the two continued on their walk.

"God must truly be with us," mumbled Abe, wiping sweat from his face. The sudden appearance of the German shepherd was a total surprise. He never dreamed that such a thing could happen.

While working at the estate, Abe had helped raise him from a puppy. He was called Ajax. The dog was a gift to the SS commander at Sucha. From the day it was brought to the estate Abe had been assigned to take care of him.

Ajax developed into a vicious canine, growing to the size of a small cow. He barked and jumped, bared his fangs at everyone. Even the German staff officers feared him; they would curse him constantly. That was when Abe started to wear protective clothing and began to train the animal.

Abe would feed and walk him, and only he did not

provoke the snarling attacks. Ajax grew quite fond of the prisoner, and remained a close companion to Abe until the very day they were transferred to Radom.

"What are we supposed to do now?" grumbled Aron. "That dog knows your scent. He knows you're here."

Abe concentrated. Had Ajax persisted in his scratching, it could have spelled disaster. If the SS commander had knelt beside the dog, raised the ice cellar's hatch, they would have been found.

"We can't take any chances here." Abe told Aron. "The dog could easily arouse someone's suspicions. Luckily Ajax obeyed Petzolt's command this time. If he hadn't we'd probably be dead now."

"Then what happens next time?"

"We can't afford a next time."

Their safe hiding place had to be abandoned in a hurry. This German shepherd had suddenly become their worst enemy.

There was a fenced-in area on the grounds that was forbidden territory to all soldiers except the top echelon officers. A place from which orders were issued to soldiers fighting at the front.

They waited until nightfall. Sometime long after midnight, they hastily abandoned the ice cellar's attic. Nimbly, knowing every inch of ground, they made their way to a fence and clambered over. A little orchard was situated next to the SS headquarters building. Aron and Abe searched among the trees for a place to dig, to create a new bunker for themselves.

Two willow trees, separated by a thick patch of grass were close by. As good a place as any for their purpose, they decided.

The willows' inordinately long branches reached outward and downward, almost to the ground. The odds favoring the utilization of this location were in their favor; if their bunker was built precisely beneath the hanging branches, no one was likely to walk over it.

They crawled on their bellies to the blacksmith's shop. Breathlessly, they broke a window. Once inside the deserted shop they searched for whatever they needed. A shovel, and an assortment of small tools. They then hurried back to the orchard.

While Abe dug frantically, Aron carried away the dirt, using his jacket with the sleeves tied together to keep the soil from spilling. He spread it carefully, scattering it in various places so no signs of digging would be noticeable. They dug all night, ever alert for patrolling soldiers.

"We can't dig it very deep because water from the streams will seep in," Abe cautioned.

Nor could their bunker be made very wide because of the obstruction of the willow roots. The result was an available space not much larger than a child's cradle: a hole, one meter deep, and a meter and a half wide.

They finished their work slightly before dawn. They rushed to the lumber yard where they picked up pieces of lumber and some straw. They packed layers of wood and straw along the sides and top of the bunker. It was almost daylight now. The job was almost completed, the only thing left to do was to return to the attic to collect their few belongings.

In order to enter the bunker, they had to lie on their backs, and squirm like worms through the small opening cut at the base of the willow tree trunks. Slim as they were, they barely made it. Inside there wasn't enough room to stretch out. They were forced to lay curled on their sides in a fetal position.

"Like two herrings," Abe remarked with gallows' humor.

"Koptera will be looking for us back in the attic," reminded Aron. "We've got to find a way to let him know . . ."

It was going to be quite risky to leave their new sanctuary, but there was no choice. The next night Abe slipped back outside and made his way to Koptera's house. The puzzled Pole was told of the new danger engendered by Ajax. Koptera wanted to know where they found a new haven.

The Pole would not voluntarily turn them in, Abe was sure. But it was possible that should the Germans suspect him of harboring Jews, he'd be tortured until he betrayed them. Therefore, Abe did the only thing he could, in such a situation; he lied, telling Koptera that they had gone deep into the forest, about four kilometers from the castle.

For one last time the cordial Koptera gave them food. Now they would no longer be able to go back to him for help. With the increasing number of soldiers in the area, it was too dangerous for everyone involved. Koptera had to be kept out of harm's way.

While it was still summer there wouldn't be too much of a hardship in finding food. They could steal fresh vegetables and fruits from the garden. Dry beans in the sun. Forage in the fields or woods when the opportunity presented itself.

However, the problem of the German shepherd dog remained. Every time Ajax went anywhere near the orchard he would start barking and wouldn't stop.

"I've got to find a way to keep him quiet," said Abe. "If I could get him to play with me, lick me, he'd probably stop becoming so agitated all the time."

135

They waited for an opportunity. Once again it was risky, but they had to take the chance.

Near the great house was a tennis court. Ajax was kept there at night. The dog ate far better than the miserable food they fed to Jews and other laborers in the work camps. The dog would frequently be seen chewing on a bone.

Abe slipped out of the bunker in the dark and headed for the tennis court. He crept as close to the sleeping dog as he dared. From the other side of the fence he whispered the dog's name.

"Ajax! Ajax!"

Ajax opened half-closed eyes. He wagged his tail as he sniffed Abe's scent and bounded to his feet.

Abe quietly opened the fence door to the tennis court. The German shepherd bounded through gleefully. The huge canine jumped on his old friend and licked his face. Abe petted and calmed the animal. Then he led Ajax into the fields for a midnight walk. He picked apples from the trees and uprooted and gathered as many vegetables as he could carry. The dog leaped happily beside him. Soon Abe brought him back to the tennis court, petted him again, and returned to the bunker. After that night, Ajax would no longer bark or growl when he passed the orchard.

The summer passed, and colder weather set in. It would not be possible to steal food from the fields much longer. Again they were forced to make urgent decisions. They might return to their only ally, Koptera, but decided against it because it was becoming riskier.

Aron thought long and hard. Where to go now? What to do?

"Do you remember our neighbor in Bialobrzegi, Jan Jarzobek?"

"Yes," said Abe.

"Jarzobek was always good to us. After Papa and the others were taken away, it was Jan who told me what happened. I think we should go to see him."

"Return to Bialobrzegi, Aron? Are you forgetting the main road to Warsaw? It passes right by the town. Military Police are constantly on guard. Do you have any idea how many convoys must be travelling to the front?"

Aron knew the answer quite well. It was one of the chief reasons they never dared to undertake a journey to their home, even as close to Sucha as it was.

"We'll starve or freeze to death if we stay in this bunker," he reminded his skeptical brother. "And don't forget how much Jan used to care about me. His son and I were the best of friends. I always helped them with their harvests. Jan's never turned me away before."

"Neither had Itzhak's friends," said Abe scornfully. "what makes you think he'll be different?"

"I have a feeling about Jan. I don't believe he'll turn us in, or even throw us out. In any case, he'll certainly help us find food." Aron waited while Abe mulled over the idea.

Impatiently, Aron added, "Papa trusted him. Jan always kept his word with us. Anyway, can you suggest a better idea?"

No, he couldn't, Abe realized. Koptera had helped them; it was possible that a lifelong friend such as Jan might do likewise. Perhaps Aron was right after all. Abe felt compelled to relent. Time was running out. Winter would soon become their latest enemy. Already accustomed to living a daily existence of extreme danger, he at last agreed. They would return to Bialobrzegi.

They filled flour bags with onions, cabbages, and potatoes taken from the field. This was as much as they could manage to carry. They would bring this to their old friend; and pray he wouldn't refuse to help them as so many others had.

Chapter Fourteen

"Someone is tapping on the window."

Jan Jarzobek emptied his wide-bowled pipe and looked at his wife. "Why don't you ask who it is?"

"It's almost one o'clock in the morning."

Jan rose from his chair to his full height. He turned the kerosene lamp down quite low. The windows were covered with old newspapers, keeping as much light as possible from showing outside. Any illumination might attract Allied bombers. The front had come closer than ever with artillery fire becoming a way of life. Battle-steeled German Panzer convoys moved virtually uninterrupted twenty four hours a day along the heavily traveled Warsaw-Radom road. A desperate effort was expended to fortify bombarded, crucial Nazi positions. The concentration of heavy Russian artillery thundered from over the horizon in frightening response to the armored build-up.

"Who is it? Who's out there?" the woman asked worriedly.

Aron heard her, and replied, "It's me, Aron. Mosca's son . . ."

Aron, thought Jan. Young Aron Goldfarb? Could it be? Was it possible?

At the mention of his mother's name, Aron heard Jan excitedly shout to his wife, "You don't know Aron?" he exclaimed. "What are you waiting for? Why don't you open the door?"

The whitewashed wooden door swung wide. Yellow lamplight bathed the brisk night air. The two brothers hurried inside the warm cottage. The room they entered was exactly as Aron had remembered it, right down to the faded photograph of Jan's family on the mantle. He glanced at the familiar picture, thinking it seemed a lifetime ago since he had last been here.

Jan's wife drew back in horror at the sight of the ragged, dirty and emaciated youths standing disconsolately before her. Their seedy appearance was shocking and upsetting.

Jan stood there staring at them with his jaw agape. He could not believe it either. His lower lip began to quiver, and unexpectedly he began to cry.

He opened his arms to Aron, embraced him tightly, and kissed him on both cheeks. "My God, Aron, you're alive. *Alive.*" Then wiping his eyes, he drew back and took another look at his unexpected guests.

After shutting the door, he said, "Sit, sit, please." He beckoned to both young men to make themselves comfortable, then he motioned to his wife. "Bring them something to eat for heaven's sake," he told her.

Aron and Abe sat down on the old worn chairs. "We've so many things to tell you, Jan . . ."

The farmer raised his hand, stopping Aron. "Those

140

things can wait for a while. First have something to eat. You both look starved."

A supper of bread, cheese and fruit was served, along with a pot of steaming fresh tea. They stared at the food that Jan's comely wife placed in front of them. To the fugitives this meager meal was a veritable feast. Gratefully, Abe and Aron ate voraciously. A second helping was quickly devoured.

When they were finished Jan eagerly sat to listen; their plight was obvious to him, though the details needed to be filled in.

"Where have you two been hiding?" he asked.

Still wary of finding themselves betrayed, even by such a close friend, Aron replied reticently, "We've been deep in the woods, in the back hills where the Germans or the AK can't find us."

Jan nodded gloomily. He was certainly aware of the atrocities being committed. Terrible acts, barbaric and cruel, without justification.

Jan's wife poured the tea. Aron sipped his slowly, savoring every drop. He couldn't remember how long it had been since he last drank real tea.

Jan then offered them a pack of cigarettes, and Aron took one eagerly. He lit up, and gave another to Abe. Aron inhaled long and deeply. Blue smoke rose toward the ceiling as he blew it upward.

In the distance heavy mortar shells screeched and exploded. Jan turned out the lamp. "It's going from bad to worse," he muttered. "Germans, Russians, razing the land. Our land. Fighting their battle over our beloved soil."

The Poles were becoming increasingly uneasy. The threat of the Red Army posed a greater to them than the Nazi invasion. Many believed if the conquering Germans had brought Poland to its knees, then

141

another invader, the feared Soviets, would cripple their homeland forever. Aron was well aware of this alarm and the growing panic the war had recently caused.

"Please, go on," Jan said after the bombardments abated.

In the dark of his parlor the escapees started to re-count their story, and told of the dreadful extermination of so many of their people. Jan, however, wanted only to hear about the fate of the Jewish family he had befriended so many years ago.

Aron spoke first, trying to explain their most abandoned moments, how they lived so precariously close to death at the hands of the Germans, and their bold escape from Pionki. He also related how they had been turned away time after time by those upon whom they had counted most, and how this had torn Itzhak apart.

Jan listened intently and sadly at the news of Itzhak's death. He vividly remembered the day pretty Mosca Goldfarb gave birth to her first child, her first son, and named him Itzhak. Issaac, son of Abraham, of the Old Testament. And how proud Moshe, the rabbi, Jan's neighbor and good friend, had been to have a son. He recalled how much the father had loved the boy.

Again tears welled in his weary eyes. He wiped them away.

"I'm glad you came to me," said Jan at length. He looked fixedly at Aron. "You know how much I love you, Aron. Almost as if you were my own son." Then he gazed downward, ashamedly. "But you are also aware of what would happen to my own family if—"

"I understand," said Aron, interrupting the farmer. Both the Germans and the AK would slaughter them all, and burn down his little farm if they suspected Jews were being concealed with his knowledge.

142

Jan saw their disappointment and started to weep again. "What has this world come to?" he said sadly. "Why must a man turn away those he loves?"

When he wiped his eyes for the second time, he said in a low tone, "Listen to me, both of you. Do either of you recall where we used to cut the hay? If you wish, you can hide in the haystacks. I will bring you food, you have my word on it."

Aron shook his head. He reached out and put his hand on the farmer's shoulder. "Thank you for wanting to help, Jan, but no, we can't accept. We already do have a place. But we could use the food, especially now that winter is almost here."

"You come here, then. You come to me. Whatever I have, whatever my family can spare, consider it yours." Jan spoke with such open honesty, such genuine kindness. Aron had all but forgotten that emotions such as these could still exist. He held the farmer close to him, fighting off his own emotional surge.

For a brief moment, in the darkness, they all wept.

Aron knew he would never—could never—forget this farmer's kindness. After such a long time, so many lonely, desperate months and years, at last there was someone who had held out a hand in friendship to them. A simple gesture of decency and empathy from one human being to another. No, Aron knew he'd never forget this wonderful moment. Moreover, should the day ever come when he could repay this kindness, he surely would.

With these feelings of gratitude they left Jan's house in the way they came, under cover of darkness.

On their way back to the bunker they passed the little wooden cottage where they had been raised. In his mind's eye Aron could see Papa standing sternly at the door, pocket watch in hand, looking on as the processsion of his Hebrew school students filed quietly out after class. He could also see lovely, young Brucha laughing and playing on the grass with her toddler brother, Simon. Then suddenly there was Ester before him; sweet, kind-hearted Ester, standing at the stove, pushing back her long red hair, an apron around her waist, calling everyone to supper.

Ghosts of his past, but alive within his mind and soul.

While I survive, they survive, he told himself. *Within me, they live.*

The terrible yearning for his family ached within him—a need to be with all of them, and to hear their voices again; share their fate. The black void occasioned by their absence shattered him. Nor did spoken words of this filial love have to be shared with Abe. Lost in his own fond memories, the older youth also felt a painful longing for the family he held so dear.

The two brothers wept silently as they went on their way. It was a very long and lonesome walk back to their current home: a shallow hole dug into the ground.

The orchard at Sucha was in a closed, off-limits area. SS orders stated, that with the exception of the gardener, no one was allowed to trespass. Because of this seclusion it became possible for them to establish a routine. Each day, as they lay in the bunker, they discussed plans for the oncoming night. Then, forced to live as nocturnal creatures, they would slip out of their burrow and scavenge for food. Anything they could find that was edible.

Anyone who caught sight of the duo would have thought that they were wild men, escaped lunatics from some mental institution. They were squalid, and threadbare. Barely appearing human, risking life itself for a potato, or a rotting apple. Any bit of nourishment to help them survive for one more day.

Weeks passed, becoming months. The war closed in on them, Sucha became busy issuing frantic directives to the arriving German divisions.

It was already autumn. The relentless wind grew colder, blowing down from the snow-capped mountains. Abe, with Aron's help, would steal into the ice cellar to seek pieces of meat. On one particular chilly night as Abe eased himself down to the cellar's floor the layer of ice cracked and gave way. Abe toppled in a mudslide.

Aron quickly took hold of the brittle wooden slats and dropped to the bottom. Abe sat in pain.

"Is anything broken?" asked Aron, cradling his brother.

Abe shook his head, rubbing his aching legs. "I don't think so. I didn't realize the ice would be so thin."

"Let me see."

"No time for that now. Let's find what we can, and get out of here."

They rummaged, picking up whatever might be useful. Abe found a frozen slice of beef, Aron took an empty milk can. There were some vegetables, and fresh water.

Climbing back out, they hurried to the safety of the forest. They pooled their meager resources, filled the milk can with some water, vegetables and fatty meat. Abe started a small fire, and they cooked a stew.

Mouths watering, they ate quickly, savoring every morsel. However, their stomachs weren't accustomed to such food. The meat was slightly tainted, and both became ill.

They hoped that the remainder of the meat could be saved for another time. They placed it into the milk can and tied it high to a tree branch. They returned the next day. The milk can had mysteriously disappeared. Stolen not by fellow scavengers, they were sure, but by more insidious enemies with whom they had been battling for a long time. Rats.

In their bunker, when one of them slept, the other remained awake, watching out for the disease-carrying rodents.

Moreover, field mice burrowing in the orchard had made tunnels in the hay and sand around the bunker. Before long the mice had moved inside. Within a matter of weeks literally dozens were scurrying in and out of the underground shelter the brothers had so painstakingly built. They had no choice but to live with them.

Disgusted at first, as time passed both Aron and Abe no longer attempted to fend them off. Trying to keep them out had proved useless in any case. They had no other option but to get used to the sight of them. Even to accept the mice. Yet, in time the mice fled, replaced by their larger and more dangerous cousins, the rats. Some grew as large as cats. Running across the ceiling of the bunker, scurrying over the papers Abe had placed there to keep dirt from falling into their eyes.

On many a day as Aron lay there in silence he could see their shadows as they raced back and forth in groups. Using a glass bottle as a weapon, Aron killed as many as he could. But they came in even greater numbers, becoming a constant menace until their very lives were threatened.

The rats ate the shoelaces of their shoes. And then, while the brothers slept, they would nibble at the leather of the soles of their shoes. They chewed holes in Abe's beret as he lay resting. They clawed the inviting human hair. On many occasions Aron was wakened by rats scampering over his feet. It was a continual struggle. A war within a war. And one that challenged their intelligence and cunning to win.

Would a day ever come when they would be able to leave this living tomb? At times it seemed hopeless.

There was a road at the far edge of the orchard. During daylight hours they could hear the wagons rolling, and frequently even the talk of nearby farmers. They strained to hear what was being said.

Were the Germans losing the war? Did the Allies make more inroads against them? Had the poorly-armed Russians broken the Eastern Front at last, or had the Red Army been pushed back?

Only the thought and hope of possible liberation kept them alive. It had to happen, they believed. Bombings were becoming routine, the Nazis were hard pressed to fight on so many fronts. Their empire was definitely collapsing.

These matters, though, seemed of little interest to the local farmers as they paused on the road. All Aron could overhear was gossip about neighborhood folk.

Each day two Poles who worked in the nearby fields would come to the road with their horse-drawn carts and stop to have a conversation. One was always regaling the other with graphic descriptions of his amatory feats in bed with his wife. The other would listen and then they would both laugh. Aron was revolted by them.

What ignorant fools, these were. The world around them was subjected to the most horrible destruction ever known. Poland was a shambles, occupied, beaten, beset by enemies from without and within. Tens of thousands of their own Christians had been slaugh-

147

tered, as well as millions of innocent Polish Jews. These were the greatest crimes against humanity. These two laborers though didn't seem to care about anything but women and drinking. It infuriated Aron.

One day, Aron told himself, *we will be free. And on that day I will teach these barbarians a lesson they will not soon forget.*

Inside the bunker, as they fought the rats and passed time, they made good use of anything and everything that might be found. Tin cans proved to be especially useful. Not only could items be stored in them, but they could utilize them for cooking pots. On one chilly night they came across an empty five-gallon petrol can, discarded apparently by the Germans. That became their urinal. They kept it tightly closed always because uncovered the stench became nauseating. Several weeks later when the can had been filled, the brothers thought of another use for it.

Moving from the bunker, they carried the urine-filled improvised portable latrine to the middle of the road and left it there, certain that on the following day the two gossiping Poles would be sure to come by and find it.

When morning came, Aron and Abe, huddled safely in their underground refuge, listened for them. They weren't disappointed.

They heard the hoof beats of the horse's clopping on the road, as well as the squeaking of the wagon wheels.

"Whoa!" cried one of the laborers, pulling back the reins. He leaned over the buckboard and stared in wonder. "I think I found something," he said to his friend.

Both workers jumped from the wagon and hurried to see what it was. "A can of petrol! The Germans lost a can of petrol!" They were ecstatic. Then they started to argue over which of them would get the prize.

"I saw it first," said one.

"No you didn't," replied the other.

It was one of the few moments in Aron's life when he was able to smile. The workers carried on aggressively about the rightful owner of the find. Unable to decide which of them would keep it, they agreed to open the can, perhaps to split up the valuable fuel between them.

Aron could hear as one of the laborers removed the lid. The stink must have sent them reeling. "It's a petrol bomb!" One of them shouted. "Run!"

And run they did, leaving the spilled can in the middle of the road. Aron and Abe laughed uproariously.

They soon found a way to add a new supplement to their poor diet. With some flour they might be able to make bread or flour cakes. Staples they might be able to store for some time to help them through the winter's hardships. The next project they decided to undertake would be a raid on Sucha's flour mill. Though guards were ever present around the area of the mill, they knew their way well enough to avoid them.

Aron slipped out first with Abe right behind. Reaching the old mill, he broke a pane of glass in a small window and squeezed his way inside. Abe took the sacks of flour one at a time as Aron hurriedly passed them on to him. They then hid most of the sacks in the attic above the ice cellar.

They carried some back to the bunker where they spent the next day making dough from a mixture of flour and water. The following night they came across

149

a metal can which they quickly converted into a sort of stove. Out in the woods they cooked as many flat pancakes as they could.

"Fine looking cakes," Aron said with pride with they were finished. There were dozens of them. So many in fact, that they were unable to carry all of them back.

They packed as many as possible inside the bunker, expecting them to last for weeks. The flour cakes, however, had not been properly baked. They were raw inside, and within a few days they became moldy. This caused the problem of disposing of them.

The nights were becoming colder. Soon the frigid winter would set in. Bundled in their jackets, they would leave their refuge at about midnight, walk into the dense woods surrounding the castle, and search for additional provisions. The orchard featured an abundance of fruit trees, but unfortunately most were saplings, too young to bear fruit. Out in the fields, though, they would find enough onions and potatoes to help them survive. They ate a few, and stored the remainder in the ice cellar.

At night the woods were very cold. Aron sat close to the small fire they started among the clusters of spruce and tall evergreens. They warmed their hands over the fire. Orange-colored flames danced before Aron's eyes, and embers crackled loudly. The heat of the fire felt good. He removed his heavy jacket and hung it on a tree branch. Abe sat opposite, apportioning their meal. The ground was covered with a layer of brown fallen leaves interspersed with thistledown. Not more than thirty meters away was the clearing, sloping down to the fields. The lights of the village glimmered dimly, reflecting a panoramic, peaceful scene.

150

They ate silently and were somber and reflective. Wind rustled through the branches.

Aron suddenly stopped eating and looked at his brother. "I think I just heard something."

"Like what?" Abe glanced around, his knife close at hand.

"Talking, people."

"Impossible. You're hearing things, Aron."

"No. I'm not. Be quiet and listen."

"Your nerves are jumpy. I don't hear anything. It could be birds. Sometimes when they're far away they sound like people chatting."

An instant later the rapid fire of a machine gun could be heard. The *rat-tat-tat* impelled them to jump to their feet, and dash for the deeper cover of the forest.

Everything was left behind. Food, utensils, fresh water. Aron cursed under his breath as he realized he had also forgotten his pocketknife.

Trying to catch their breaths, they paused below the tall, thin, leafy branches of a birch tree. "We should be safe enough for the present," Aron managed to say, holding his side.

Abe agreed. Now that the immediate danger had passed, he noticed his brother, and became upset. "Where's your jacket?" he asked. "You left it back at the campfire."

All Aron could do was groan. He was getting terribly cold.

"How do you expect to survive in this weather without your jacket?"

"I—I suppose I'll have to go back and fetch it."

They waited for about an hour, then crept silently over the hard ground back to their fire. They stopped in the shadow of a huge, weather-beaten oak tree. To

151

their surprise they found that the fire had been extinguished, all the food gone, as well as his jacket. Someone had been there and took his jacket.

It posed a serious problem. The Polish winters were frigid, rivalling those in Russia. Deaths from frostbite were not uncommon. Without warm clothing Aron would be unable to leave the bunker. There would no longer be any forays into the forests. It was already insufferably cold, and the worst part of winter had not yet arrived.

Life was becoming more intolerable. The brothers managed to start a small fire inside the bunker for cooking. They left the hole above the flames open to prevent their suffocation. Now they also ran the risk of the smoke being noticed by anyone passing the orchard.

They knew that there was no possible way they could continue on like this. Dangerous as it was, Abe knew he would have to return to the farmer who had first given them food, the Christian Koptera.

Chapter Fifteen

Aron had no watch, no way of knowing what time it was. How long had it been since Abe left him alone to go to see Koptera? An hour? It felt as though a thousand nights had passed. His heartbeat increased dramatically. Restlessly he twisted and turned in the safety of the narrow, stifling bunker.

How much longer?

Stay calm, he told himself. *All's well, Abe is well. He'll be back soon. He promised he would.*

It was about three or four hours since his brother had left. However long, though, it had been interminable. His mind was reeling, tortured by the fear of being alone in this rat-infested hellhole.

Ever since Itzhak's tragic death, he and Abe had clung to one another almost fanatically. A bonding of two brothers who had lost so much. In this insane world of cruelty Abe was the only one that Aron had left. Together they might be able to carry on, day after day after brutal day, as a unit. An entity. The remnants of a family. But to have to face it all alone . . . ?

No, Aron was sure that he could never make it alone. *He should have returned already. Where is he?*

Fear gripped him. His thoughts were ominous. What if Abe had run into the AK as Itzhak had, and what if they shot him also. Would he, once again, hear that yet another young Jew had been found and murdered?

The thought made him shudder. It would be too much to bear. He might as well be dead too. In death's eternal embrace he would at last find peace.

He became angry with himself for even contemplating such macabre and appalling possibilities. What was wrong with him?

Aron prayed as Papa had taught him. His mind, however, kept returning to the same ghastly thoughts.

Dead. All of them dead. The whole world was dead, razed right before his eyes as in an *Inferno* that wasn't a dream. Only he and Abe remained alive. And now, perhaps, only himself. Alone.

Unable to bear the torture of waiting he prepared to leave the bunker. He knew that it was probably a foolhardy move but he couldn't help himself. Abe had left to see Koptera at about eleven o'clock. Judging by the stars Aron estimated the time to be between two and three in the morning. He hastily wrapped flour bags around himself to fight off the bitter cold, and went out into the bitter night to begin his search.

He crawled along the recently harvested field on hands and knees. Dried remains of sunflower seeds scraped his legs, rubbing into his flesh along with the dirt, stinging his skin. The wind howled through the rushes, frigidly and savagely goading and taunting him, making him struggle for every centimeter of land he traversed.

Enemies were all around him. Rats in the field.

154

Germans on patrol. AK thugs prowling the hills. Hunger gnawing at his belly. Glacial cold freezing his body.

God, he cried, *have you abandoned me?*

Frantic, he knew he had to keep going. He had to find Abe no matter what the cost.

An owl hooted, its haunting cry echoed across the desolate, lonely field. Aron shivered. Was this nocturnal creature another portent of things to come? He remembered the flock of blackbirds, and the superstitions surrounding them.

No, he would repel this pessimism. He would not give up his struggle to survive, *never.*

His breathing became slow and labored. The horror of his life was overwhelming, catapulting him into an abyss from which he could not extricate himself.

Images flashed across his mind. Papa, bending over the stove, stoking the fire. Mama in the kitchen drying her hands while Brucha and Ester laughed merrily along with her.

What had become of them all? He cried out to himself in anguish. What had become of him? Slinking like a wild beast in a morass, freezing on his hands and knees, hiding like a hunted creature. He was bereft of everything including his humanity. Was life itself merely a cruel hoax devised by some unrelenting deity?

Had God really abandoned him? He kept asking himself the same question over and over again.

Papa would be ashamed to hear his question now, he realized. How dare he even doubt—no matter the adversity.

There is but one God. . . .

Aron wept. Teardrops froze on his cheeks but he did not feel them.

Moonlight beamed in lustrous silvery rays, illuminating the parameters of the field. Aron crouched lower, simultaneously moving forward. The paper sack tied over his underwear severely scratched his stomach. Before leaving, Abe had borrowed Aron's tattered clothes to keep him warm during his journey to Koptera.

Even though they had been nothing but old rags, another layer would still be helpful. Although Abe hadn't spoken of it, he was reasonably certain that if Aron had no protection against the night then his younger brother would be forced to remain in the bunker. Aron realized this, yet he could not remain behind. Not again. Not any more.

Aron heard a rustling nearby. He froze, laying motionless in the dirt. Wild pigs were rooting for food, grunting the same way they did during the night Itzhak was killed. This was another omen, Aron was sure.

He kept forcing himself to move on. His mind was made up: He would go directly to Koptera—and should he learn that Abe had been killed, he would give up the struggle. Commit suicide. Abandoned and alone, his life was not worth living.

At length he crossed the harvested tract. He rose, running amid the clumps of large, stately oaks and birch trees that were blocking his path. The undergrowth scratched his calloused heels and his ankles, drawing blood. He trod over thorns and acorns, his face red from exertion, muscles straining, his body aching all over and numbed by the sub-zero weather. Only the quickened beating of his heart assured him he had enough stamina left for at least one more step.

He was nearing the village, and Koptera's cottage. The little stone bridge spanning calm waters stood before him. He composed himself. Whatever the truth, he would soon find out.

A shadow appeared on the far side of the quaint bridge. Aron dropped to the ground, holding his breath as he lay prone, watching. As the darkened figure drew closer Aron recognized Abe.

Aron rose.

Abe stared at the pitiful figure wrapped in flour bags, and grinned. They approached each other and embraced. In the moonlight, Aron could see that Abe too was now overcome with emotion. Dirt mingled with his tears as they coursed down his face. He could not believe that his younger brother had come out in this bitter weather almost naked, to look for him. The sight of Aron left him shaken. He quickly covered Aron with as many clothes as he could. Then he explained why he had been delayed.

"I accomplished everything I set out to do," he began. "Koptera gave me some food, cigarettes, even matches. I was already on my way back to the bunker, crossing the woods, when I spotted a German platoon hiding among the trees. I don't know where they came from. They seemed to appear out of nowhere."

"A German platoon here?"

Abe nodded. "I saw trucks, armored cars, artillery, and all kinds of equipment. Before I could turn around, one of the soldiers saw me and shouted for me to halt. I had no choice. His rifle was aimed straight at me. 'Raise your hands,' he ordered, so I obeyed. Two Germans looked me over very carefully.

"'What are you doing here so late at night?' they barked. I shrugged, and spoke in my best Polish, trying not to appear to frightened. Looking at my watch, I answered, 'It's only eight-thirty. The curfew doesn't start until nine.'

"They muttered to themselves in German, not realizing, of course, how well I understood the language. They apparently didn't know what time it was. My

157

guess had been right. One soldier asked his commanding officer, 'What shall we do with him?' The officer said, 'Let the Polish pig go.'"

Abe had called their bluff on the curfew, and miraculously he won.

"So I walked straight through their lines," Abe continued, "came to this bridge so badly shaken I was sure that I was done for. When they let me go I was really surprised. They could have killed me right there, or worse, brought me to headquarters for questioning." He smiled. "I guess I was just lucky, it wasn't my time to die."

No, it wasn't, Aron thought. God does exist after all.

Chapter Sixteen

It was December of 1944. Winter had arrived in all its fury. The cold was merciless. The orchard and fields were frozen. Their food supply was completely exhausted, and they were starving.

Debilitated, unnerved, enervated and *in extremis,* Abe decided to do what he vowed he never would: visit Koptera one more time. Only now the chances for success were far worse than before. The German Army was on the move everywhere. Soviet mobile battalions were attacking Nazi forces on all fronts. War-weary German troops cluttered the streets of the villages, confiscated homes, expropriated food. Their supply vehicles clogged the busy roads, troops setting up makeshift camps as they waited to return to the raging disarrayed front to face the Russian onslaught.

Unaware of it, the noose around the Third *Reich* was rapidly tightening. Persisting in overruling the opposition of his general staff, Hitler had stubbornly demanded total resistance from his depleted armies. German forces were now faced not only with the Red Army's counteroffensive, but the total inability of the *Luftwaffe* to control the skies. Radio Moscow had for months been broadcasting in Polish to the Poles calling for a general uprising. The winter offensives of 1944 were underway.

Outside of Koptera's house, Abe waited in the icy cold. He peered through the foggy window as Koptera and his family prepared to retire. In the cottage next door a group of billeted soldiers were bedding down for the night as well.

When all lights were extinguished in both houses, and he was reasonably sure of not being seen, Abe rapped on the frozen window in the signals he and the farmer had long ago devised. While working at Sucha, Abe always stole extra food for the Pole and his family, and now he was grateful that these good deeds were being repaid. Koptera alone stood between them and catastrophe.

Koptera's sharp eyes darted to and fro. When he too believed it was safe, he motioned for Abe to come to the front of the house. Abe entered through the slightly opened door. In the dark Koptera winced at the sight of his friend. "My God, Abe, what's the matter?"

Frozen, hands clenched and barely able to move, Abe weakly managed to say, "Aron and I have big problems. I don't believe we'll be able to survive."

Koptera despondently placed his arm around the fugitive. He asked him to sit, then scrounged for some food, a few cigarettes to take back to the bunker.

"Abe, my good friend," he said with a sigh, "sometimes things go well, at other times they go badly. But be assured of one thing: If you've made it this far, you'll live to see this bloody war end." Koptera gritted his teeth. As the Third *Reich* became more disheartened, their iron-fisted rule over Poland became more intolerable. Christian Poles were being imprisoned and shot by the thousands. There had been wanton looting and pillaging in the towns and cities, even mindless massacres and rapes. As many as two hundred thousand were reported dead in Warsaw alone, after Hitler had ordered the total destruction of the capital. The Nazi situation was desperate.

"You're young, Abe," Jan stressed, aware of the suffering his friend was enduring. "You have your whole life. You have your brother." He handed Abe the package he'd prepared for him.

"Have patience, my friend. Don't return because it's too dangerous for you. Hope that the war will be over very soon."

Abe's eyes brightened. "What's the latest news you've heard?"

"The Nazis are in disarray. The Americans and British are nearing the Rhine, they say. Churchill is broadcasting that the end is in sight. Rumors say the Allies will not stop until they take Berlin. There is word of Field Marshal Montgomery's and General Patton's victories on Germany's borders. The Russians are no longer stalled; they've broken through at every point at last. The entire Eastern Front has collapsed for the Germans. Hitler has his hands full, I tell you. Everywhere his armies are in retreat. They are panicking."

"Koptera," said Abe, sighing, "you've given me hope for the first time in a long while. You've given me a new life."

The good news was greeted joyously in the little bunker. Nevertheless, neither brother knew just when the Red Army's final breakthrough might come, and

Poland at long last, liberated. Meanwhile, winter had arrived, and the scraps of food Koptera had been able to spare were hardly enough to sustain them.

"Where do you think you're going?" said Abe later as Aron prepared to leave.

"Get up, too. We're heading for Coming." It was the tiny village near the castle. "There's a Pole there I know. Maicher, by name. We worked together at Sucha. I know his daughters, and his entire family. It's worth a shot."

Abe was dubious. "Be careful, Aron. He's not one to trust."

Aron smiled. "Don't worry, we'll take care."

Now it was his turn to evade the enemy. The treacherous journey to Coming did not take long. They found the house of his former friend, and Aron knocked on the window.

"Maicher, are you there?"

No answer.

"Maicher, it's Aron. We used to work together at the great estate, remember? I need some food. A few cigarettes, if you can spare them."

It took a while for the rugged-featured Pole to come to the window. "I don't want you here," he said belligerently. "I have no food or cigarettes to give you. Nothing. Now get the hell away from my house!"

Aron felt his anger rising.

No longer would he run like a thief in the night. No more would be beg or plead for a crumb. He had as much right to live as any man. He was a human being with dignity.

"Listen to me, Maicher," he hissed. "And listen well. I need food and cigarettes. I'm not playing games. Give it to me or I'll burn down you house with you in it."

Again there was no response.

"Don't wait for him, Aron," said Abe, loudly enough

162

for Maicher to hear. "Light your matches right now. Smash the window, throw them inside and burn this damned house down to the ground."

Maicher became frightened. These hunted Jews were crazy and capable of any heinous act.

He tossed out some bread and a half empty packet of cigarettes. The brothers took their prize and moved out into the silent night.

Aron didn't have a single match. He'd been bluffing all the way. But desperate men take desperate measures.

Together in the bunker they lay still, dozing on and off. Outside, a vicious wind howled furiously.

Aron lay on his side, listening.

"Are you awake?"

"Yes."

"We won't make it, will we?"

He considered it for a while. They were growing weaker every day. The winter hampered their movements. Snow covered the barren fields. During summer, at least, they'd been able to forage. Not now, though. They had run out of places to go, friends to visit. Inside the bunker the temperature was about zero. They had few clothes, and nothing to eat. They became wild animals again, trapped and caged, and unable to move. The critical situation for the Germans, activity at Sucha worsened.

Aron listened to every sound. He wondered when the soldiers would finally find them.

After all this time it appeared that their luck had run out.

"You know, Abe, we've been chased and shot at so many times, I don't think I have any courage or belief left."

"We have to try to believe, Aron. Even if it's only in each other."

"I know. But even when I hear a stray dog barking I

163

feel a little envious, jealous because at least the dog is free to roam, to hunt, to live." Dejectedly, he closed his eyes and added, "But we're denied what even a dog is allowed."

"We will be free men again, Aron, *believe*, we will be." No assurance sounded in Abe's normally firm baritone voice. His tone betrayed his overwhelming pessimism.

It wasn't easy to have faith in anything any longer. Ruefully, Aron's thoughts turned to his brother, Jacob. It *was* possible that he was still alive, somewhere in Russia, since 1941. If he were, at least one member of the family would be assured of surviving this horror. One of them might live to marry someday, raise a family of his own, and carry on Papa's name, traditions and legacy.

It was almost Christmas. Although they were unaware of it, coincidently it was the same time that American General George Patton's renowned Third Army was smashing its way to victory and the liberation of Bastogne. For Aron and Abe, though, this was the worst winter of their lives. Temperatures outside frequently dropped to twenty degrees below zero. The landscape barren over old and new growth, and meadow alike. The countryside of hills and mountains silent from the baseline to their snow capped peaks. It was a world of ice and snow. A glistening mosaic, desolately beautiful with breathtaking natural wonder, but awesome and unforgiving to two hungry youths with no place to go; not even the howling of wolves to keep them company.

With the hatch tightly shut they managed to contain the extreme cold outside of the bunker. At night they would scoop up a pail of snow and wait for it to melt. At least they always had a supply of fresh drinking water.

164

The war crisis deepened. More and more Poles were being forced to take German soldiers into their homes, those who had come back from the enveloping front. Aron and Abe of course had no calendar, and no idea of which day or date it was. They hadn't spoken with Koptera for about a month or communicated with anyone, so it was impossible for them to know what recent events were taking place in Europe. At best they could only guess. But if the closeness of the artillery fire was any indication, then the Red Army was well within reach of victory indeed.

As Papa had taught him, Aron once more turned to prayer for solace. As he intoned the Hebrew prayers he recalled Papa's words.

Go, my son. Maybe you will survive.

Papa had told him that. It was his legacy now. His solemn obligation. His duty to do as Papa asked.

God, give me that strength Papa so wanted for me.

He prayed for the souls of Mama, Ester, Brucha, Simon, and Itzhak. Most of all, though, he prayed for Papa. Since all of them were gone, Aron felt it was incumbent upon him to perpetuate the family name, to bear the burden and lead them in Papa's direction. How could he do that now?

The wind rose in velocity and it snowed. A blizzard screeched above them. As the storm raged they heard a sudden thumping sound around them. At first Aron believed it was the wind. Soon it became obvious that the strange noises emanated not from nature, but was man-made.

The Germans were working all around their bunker.

They wondered what was happening, what the enemy was doing. But they dared not peek outside; soldiers were certain to spot them. At last, when darkness fell, Abe opened the hatch to collect some snow for drinking water, and took a quick look around. The

165

snow was several feet high piled up in all directions. He couldn't risk standing and walking because his tracks in the snow would be a certain giveaway. Instead he crawled his way up the white mound, and stopped. He stared in disbelief.

Moments later he scrambled back inside and shut the hatch. "We have to get out of here," he said shakily. "Tonight, as fast as we can."

"Why? What did you see?"

"Hear me, we can't stay here for even one more day."

Bewildered, Aron said, "Where will we go? There's a blizzard. It's too cold, and we have no adequate clothing . . ."

"We have no choice," his brother snapped. "the Germans are digging holes all around us, placements for anti-aircraft guns not three meters from our bunker."

Aron put on the thin clothes Abe had improvised for him out of the flour sacks. Bones clinging to their flesh, the brothers opened the hatch and slid out into the blustery night. The wind almost blew them down. Aron wasn't able to walk straight. Abe helped him along as much as he could, but the older of the two was showing signs of weakness from malnutrition.

The plans they'd devised were risky gambles at best.

Under the blanket of driven snow they laboriously made their way to the blacksmith's shop. Their bodies were weak, their hearts troubled, and their minds confused. Yet in times of life-threatening danger, they found renewed courage and strength. Earlier, whenever things were at their lowest ebb, they would somehow reach inside the depths of their being to draw upon their reservoir of stamina and will-power. Now, even under these harrowing conditions, with the enemy surrounding them, they felt no fear. Only a commitment to what *must* be done.

166

Calmly Aron wrapped a flour sack around his frozen hand and broke two small window panes and climbed inside. He gathered shovels, picks, and anything else they would need to build a new bunker, one situated deep in the forest and a good distance away from the German fortifications.

Had the weather been clear and warmer they might easily have been spotted by passing troops. The difference now was that they did not care. To remain meant certain death, either at the hands of the enemy, or by freezing.

Shivering in the twenty-below-zero weather, ill from hunger, they took everything they could carry and hurried towards the saw mill. Winds froze their faces and limbs. At the mill they scrounged for lumber for the new bunker. For almost two kilometers they walked in the raging storm, far enough to feel a little safer. Their hands were numb, and they were barely able to move their fingers. Yet they returned to their old shelter and carried away all they had left. A few onions, a little flour, empty but useful tins. They worked all through the night.

The sun rose at about six. They knew that they had left tracks in the fresh snow. They didn't care about that, either. They stopped feeling the cold—the first symptoms of impending frostbite. That also was not too important. Better frostbite than a Nazi bullet.

The place for the new bunker was selected, a good spot; some twenty five meters from the forest's clearing. They retraced their steps, to pick up remaining supplies. It was there that they saw the German.

"Halt!" he shouted above the wind.

He was young, this rifle-bearing soldier. Dressed warmly in his green uniform and overcoat. He aimed his weapon at the two trespassers.

Aron fled in one direction, Abe in the other. They

had long ago agreed that if they were caught they would run in opposite directions. This might help at least one of them to escape, and if not, they'd probably be shot from behind.

Aron's breathing was labored. He kept running, in spite of the pains in his gut, his bones. Rifle fire sounded close. They were chasing, and shooting at him.

He kept running, passing some Poles on their way to work on the farms. Several paused, staring. What did it matter? He ran on, dodging among the oak, birch and the pine trees. After what seemed an interminable time he spotted a large hay silo down in a field and raced toward it. He reached the silo on the verge of collapse. With every ounce of energy he could summon, he dug his hands through the icy surface of hay, hoping to dig a hole large enough in which to hide. The hay, however, had frozen over a long time ago. No matter how hard he tried he couldn't even poke a finger through. It was brick-like, solid and unyielding.

Again, the animal cunning and instinct for survival kept him alert. What to do now?

Unfortunately, there was only one option left: To return to the ice cellar's attic. Back to Sucha.

Papa, pray for me, he whispered. Then he dashed off. All the while he could hear gunfire.

The storm had abated but the weather remained unrelenting. He reached the ice cellar—within ten meters of headquarters—and wondered how he might get inside. It proved to be no easy task.

It was well past daybreak, the sky was cloudy and gray. His objective was surrounded by a cement and wooden wall five feet high. No one was going to be able to jump over it and get in. Not without being shot anyway.

Away from the wall, beyond sight of the SS head-quarters, he found the tunnel that Abe and he had dug a long time ago. He slid under the snow-covered wall, then hid among the trees, waiting for a chance to sneak into the attic. He watched soldiers moving slowly back and forth, heard the screeching of tires as jeeps struggled to move in and over the snow. Finally, the opportune moment came.

He made it into the tunnel.

He waited inside the attic. It was bitterly cold. No food or water. He was not overly concerned with these matters at the moment. All he could think of was Abe. Was he still alive, or had the German sentries shot him? Would Abe even know to look for him here?

Aron had no answer. All that day he listened to the shooting during the raging battle, and just stared from the almost iced-over window. The storm that raged only hours before was gone and it was now a beautiful day; the sky was an indigo blue, frothy white clouds drifted slowly from horizon to horizon.

At length another night arrived. Aron clasped his hands together. Worry furrowed his brows.

If my brother is still alive, he told himself, *then let him know to return to our old bunker. . . .*

Chapter Seventeen

In the snow, Abe had run along the main road that leads to Radom. How he had managed not to freeze to death was a miracle. This single day seemed endless. When his lungs were bursting and he could no longer run he jumped into a trench and covered himself with fallen branches, products of the storm. As he lay he could hear small aircraft buzzing overhead; Russian patrol planes.

His felt his heart beating furiously. Smoke could be seen rising from the nearest village. Shells whistled by all around.

Had Aron been able to escape the sentries? He asked himself over and over again. His younger brother was physically strong. Even if he did elude his pursuers how had he been able to survive this arctic weather? Only God knew. Abe had made it through this grueling time, but his half naked brother?

And if Aron is alive, where did he go?

Abe was not sure. There was no place to hide in the forest. No, Aron would have to return to some familiar place. Somewhere he could feel safe. The strong possibility of his going back to the ice cellar worried him.

Yes, he decided. If Aron were alive he *would* try to return to the ice wellar. Why? Because there was nowhere else he could go.

Abe impatiently waited for the night, when he could move about more freely. The time finally came when he succeeded in returning to the orchard at Sucha, where he crouched in the leafless bushes. He stared at the bleak tall trees with their snow-covered branches. Taking a deep breath, he began to click his tongue against his cheek; the prearranged signal between them.

Aron heard the sound. He raised his shoulders above the hatch, glanced around and saw a silhouette slinking in the snow-covered bushes. He then crawled outside and returned the signal.

When they greeted each other they were speechless. They cried and hugged. For Aron this was an unbelievably miraculous moment. They'd found each other again, and they were both unharmed.

Aron wept and prayed. He asked God's forgiveness for doubting, and thanked Him for allowing them both to survive.

In the darkness of the attic they whispered their stories; how each had been thinking only of the safety of the other. For Aron it was truly incredible. Whatever he felt all night, Abe did likewise. When Aron withstood the cold and hunger, so had Abe. Separated, they spent all those hours worrying about each other.

After a period of rest and healing, they braved the snows of winter again. They realized that the only

171

possible source of food was the German Army's garbage dump. They decided to search there.

It was quite disappointing when they found only a few pieces of stale bread, moldy, hard and inedible.

They wondered what to do next.

Inside the bunker again, Abe reached for the two small gold coins he had hidden. These were found in a pair of shoes they bought from a Christian Pole at Pionki, it was their only valuable possession.

"What are you planning to do with them?" asked Aron.

Abe shrugged. "These aren't any good to us now," he said. "I'm going to give them to Janek Koptera, along with these." He showed Aron a few faded photographs of the family; Papa, Ester, Brucha, and Simon. One picture with Jacob, and one with Itzhak. "I'll turn over everything to Koptera. Who knows how much longer the war will last. The Germans might keep fighting for months or even years. Our chances of surviving aren't very good."

"If you believe that, then why give everything to Koptera?"

Sighing, Abe replied, "because after this war *is* finally over, if anyone in our family is still alive, Koptera can find them in the villages and give them these photos. The coins will be his for this favor. At least in this way, the pictures won't be lost. Some evidence will endure to attest that all of us were once alive. A real family . . ."

Aron bowed his head sadly. His brother wanted to preserve these singular mementos of the family's existence. Each of their lives, every one of them. It had devolved to this—a handful of faded photographs.

"You know best, Abe. I won't try to dissuade you. If

you decide, for some reason, not to go, it's alright with me. We'll manage, somehow."

"No. I've been thinking it over. I have to go. There's nothing else to be done."

For kilometers around there were soldiers. Koptera was the only Pole the Germans permitted to live in the area. They found the wily farmer useful to them. So had Abe and Aron. In truth, he was now their one slim hope.

"All right, then," Aron said with resignation. "Whatever you say, I agree."

Abe told Aron to remove his clothes. He pulled them over his own to help ward off the cold. "I don't know how long this business is going to take," he said. "So stay put, all right? I don't want you moving around."

Aron promised. This time he would wait.

Many patrols crossed Abe's path from the moment he crawled out of the attic. He hid among the bushes and trees, crawling painfully to the farmer's house. What normally took ten minutes to walk now was accomplished with difficulty in hours.

To his dismay, he found that his friend was not at home. In the frigid weather Abe found refuge under tree branches and waited for Koptera to return. After some time he heard his voice. Abe looked along the icy path to the cottage. Koptera wasn't walking alone. A German soldier was escorting him.

Although the farmer had proven to be valuable to the Nazis, he wasn't completely trusted by them. They remedied this problem by not permitting him to go anywhere alone. He was constantly under guard every time he left his house.

After Koptera was safely inside his cottage, and the soldier had departed, Abe sneaked into the tiny vestibule and tapped softly on the door. It squeaked open. Koptera placed his hand over Abe's mouth before the young man could utter a word. He pulled him inside. Behind the hanging curtains in the next room Koptera's wife lay sound asleep. Janek Koptera cautioned Abe not to speak above a whisper.

The house was comfortably warm, the air filled with the pleasing aroma of freshly baked cake. Abe was hungry. When Koptera let go of him he almost collapsed.

The Pole, aghast, made the sign of the cross. He wept as he helped Abe into a chair. Then he whispered, "What's happened to you? You look as though you're at death's door."

Abe slumped wearily in the cushioned seat. Their eyes met. He held his hand to his head. "I think we've run out of luck, old friend. The Germans found and chased us. We lost everything we had. I don't know how much longer we can bear any of this. . . ."

"Stay here and don't make a sound."

The farmer moved to a small pantry while Abe watched.

He began to pack a small bundle containing pork, some bread, a few cakes that his wife had baked, and as many cigarettes as he could spare, even some shaving cream.

"You don't have enough for yourself," Abe protested, refusing to accept the package.

Koptera brushed off his protest with a wave of his big hand. "Take it. I want you to have it, and don't even try to thank me for anything."

Before accepting this generous gift, Abe took out the photographs and the gold coins that glimmered in the dim light. "I have one last favor to ask of you. Please don't refuse me, Janek. Take these pictures and hide them in some safe place. After the war, I want you to give them to any living members of my family, mementos for them to remember us. Can I count on you to do this, Janek? Will you do that much for me?"

"That *much* for you, Abe?" It was such a trifle, Koptera knew, and he nodded with conviction. "Of course I will do it. Did you have any doubts?"

"Thank you," said Abe. He was greatly relieved that his friend had not refused. "Then take these coins also, Janek. I want to give them to you. I know it isn't much, but it's all my brother and I have. Take them in payment for all your time and trouble—"

Koptera was genuinely hurt, and he showed it. "You do me an injustice, my old friend. Abe, I don't want your gold coins. I don't need them."

"I—I'm sorry, Janek . . . I didn't mean to insult you or—" He broke into tears before he could finish.

Koptera put his muscular arm around the famished youth. "Don't give up, Abe. Not now; not ever. Not after suffering so long. You *are* going to survive, I tell you. The war *is* going to end. You'll see it end, this I promise." Tears of pity for the fugitive ran copiously down his face.

"You take the gold, Janek," Abe pressed him, putting the coins firmly into the farmer's palm and closing his fingers tightly around them. "Together with the photos, all right? After the war, if you do find any survivors of my family, just remember to tell them what happened to me and Aron. That's all I'm asking of you."

"I will hold all these things for you, Abe, and when the war is over I'll return them."

The farmer handed him the package of food.

Abe gratefully took the parcel. "Thank you, Janek. Thank you for all you have done. Neither Aron nor I shall ever forget your kindness to us. . . ."

Koptera swallowed hard to keep from crying again. "Now go," he said. "Go."

Once more Abe stole away into the forbidding darkness of night.

After eating, Aron and Abe smoked a few of the cigarettes. They talked about many things through the long night. They knew that they had enough food for a few days, and this would give them enough strength to resume their foraging. If nothing else, they would return to the flour mill, break in again, and steal a few sacks to mix with water, to make a paste they could eat.

It was January, 1945. Events in Poland—and in all of Europe—were moving swiftly. The Red Army was starting its major offensive. The breach in the German front was three hundred kilometers wide. Russian spearhead units advanced relentlessly, negating Nazi resistance with powerful counterattacks.

Abe woke from an odd dream, his forehead wet with perspiration. "Aron, Aron!"

"Uh? What?" Aron woke from a deep sound sleep. "What is it?"

"Jacob, I saw Jacob in a bizarre dream. He was wearing a military uniform. Somewhere in Russia, I think. He was an officer. . . ." Abe tried to clear his head. "He's alive, Aron. I'm certain of it. And it won't be long before we see him again."

Jacob! If only Abe's dream were to come true. He took Abe's arm and squeezed it tightly. "Let's hope to God," he said. "Let's pray to God."

All through the day and night they listened to the

ceaseless artillery barrages. Huge bombs were falling closer to SS headquarters. Fierce close combat was being waged all around them. The war had reached Sucha.

"I can hear voices!" cried Aron.

But what were they saying? He strained to listen. It wasn't German or Polish that was being spoken. He looked out. Uniformed men were scurrying back and forth. They wore large fur hats. The uniforms looked strange, unlike any he had ever seen.

"Let me have a look," said Abe.

Aron moved out of the way so his brother could have an unobstructed view.

Directly in front of Abe's line of vision an officer was shouting commands to his men. A five-pointed star appeared on his fur hat. A red star.

Abe looked at his younger brother and grinned from ear to ear. "The Russians are here," he exclaimed excitedly. "Do you know what this means?"

Aron stared in disbelief.

It meant they might soon be free.

Chapter Eighteen

It was midafternoon. Aron's exhilaration knew no bounds. Everything they had been hearing, and praying for, was on the verge of happening. At last, a Nazi defeat was no longer a vague and unattainable dream; it was almost a reality.

A ferocious battle was taking place around Sucha. Soviet heavy guns were taking their toll. Advance Red Army Infantry units had penetrated the stronghold's tightly-sealed security and boundary zones. Here was the SS headquarters, the embodiment and very pulse of the vaunted German might; the critical center for this entire region of Poland and the collapsing Eastern Front.

Hand grenades were hurled across the field at the charging Russian infantrymen. Soviet soldiers instinctively lay sprawled on the ground. Earth-shattering explosions blasted the frozen terrain higher than the trees. Several Russians remained motionless and silent on the soil, while those beside them, sprinted for cover. Machine-gun fire sprayed their ranks.

From behind trees, rocks, fences, walls, and any structure affording even a minimum of cover, a barrage of rifle fire hit the German defenses. The exchange was deafening.

Somewhere in the distance, a Soviet armored vehicle creaked laboriously up an incline towards the orchard. Nazi flamethrowers pulverized it in its tracks as it reached the crest of the hill. Aron heard the screams as soldiers in a panic tried to jump out before the vehicle exploded. Many were hit by rounds of Nazi bullets. The ice and snowy earth was bloodstained. When the armored car exploded it strewed metal debris in every direction.

Vollies of mortar shells were lobbed from the Soviet side. They had fought long and hard to earn their victories and they were not about to retreat. As whistling bombs sailed overhead, Aron watched as a German machine-gun placement was blown into fragments. Like a volcanic eruption the shell devastated men and weapons. When the dust settled, dead Germans lay strewn across a section of field like limp rag dolls. One soldier's head had been blown off. Another lay legless, his boots standing upright like crimson sentinels in the bloody mud. The grisly corpses lay twisted and mangled beneath the cold winter sun.

More shouts in Russian rose above the din. A platoon of soldiers came rushing down a foothill near the road. Here and there, German snipers trying to stem the Russian advance became easy targets for the better-positioned Red Army sharpshooters. A sniper fell silently from a high tree limb. Another shrieked as a bullet smashed his face.

The battle continued to rage. In the cloudless blue

sky Soviet aircraft appeared; they swept in low to survey the battlefield. They dived and rose, tilting their wings as they were met by the constant fire of anti-aircraft guns along the perimeters of the orchard. The pounding of the guns was deafening.

Three German tanks took up fixed positions along the road to the village. Flashes of orange accompanied the fire from automatic weapons aimed at them. Cannons roared as the tanks unloosed their own deadly fusillades. Thick, dark smoke billowed ever higher. Aron could hear the screams of the wounded. The Russians strategically retreated among the burning, blackened trees.

From one side more Germans came running. From another, a squad of Soviet soldiers. They met with fixed bayonets. The skirmish was brief and bloody. Many from both sides fell as an unforeseen shell exploded during the battle. Aron couldn't tell from which side the shell was fired.

One Russian bayoneted a Nazi lieutenant. The German dropped, and as the soldier pulled his bloody bayonet from his flesh a rapid burst from another machine gun splintered him before he hit the ground. The Russian flew backward and fell lifeless, not a meter away from the enemy he'd killed only seconds before.

A bazooka shell hit the turret of one of the tanks. It smashed through the armor plates, and in front of Aron's dazed eyes the tank burst into flames. The closest tank pivoted its guns and aimed them in the direction of the woods where the bazooka had been positioned. Trees were blown high. And when the tank ceased firing a whole section of hillside was destroyed, smoldering in the ashes.

More forays followed. Fatigued, battle-scarred soldiers continued the battle. It was carnage on both sides. More men fell, some crying out, others just keeled over, lifeless.

Gradually the attacks drew to a close. Gunfire became more intermittent. And by late afternoon the orchard stood silent and serene, as if nothing had happened.

Aron looked hard at his brother. Which side had won, he wondered.

With so many casualties everywhere it was impossible to tell. He and Abe remained huddled in the attic, unsure if they should risk exposure. It wasn't until about eleven at night that they heard voices once again coming from the direction of SS headquarters. They were harsh German voices.

"Go to the right," someone was shouting.

"Shut off that light!" came another command.

"Quiet! Go that way!"

It became apparent that the Nazis were amalgamating all their remaining strength to thwart the enemy's advance. All night long Aron heard the ceaseless rumble of trucks coming and going to and from the main road. It wasn't until the next morning that there was a lull. Then, rather mysteriously, all signs of the Germans and/or the Russians disappeared.

They didn't know what had really transpired at Sucha. Had the see-saw battle come to a final resolution?

They waited with trepidation.

Sometime at about four in the afternoon noises were heard again. Now it was the Russians shouting commands to their own marching forces.

Seemingly endless streams of weary soldiers appeared and disappeared. These troop movements lasted until nightfall. The Soviets seemed to be dashing back and forth in the twilight without observable rhyme or reason.

There still was no answer to the identity of which side finally won control over the hard-fought area.

One thing, though, was certain: The Nazis were fleeing. Position after position had been crushed or abandoned. It was the end for them. Red Army forces were moving unopposed along the SS headquarters' parameters now, virtually free of enemy troops for the moment. Aron could taste freedom now.

Night came again. Abe saw several local Poles standing in a group on the deserted road. "I know one of them," he said, pointing. "He's the manager of the mill, Tromka."

Fearfully, unable to grasp the reality of what had happened, the brothers left their hiding place and made their way to the road.

Tromka immediately recognized the young men. Looking quizzically, he asked, "Did you arrive with the Russian army?"

Abe laughed at the innocent question. "No," he answered. "We didn't. My brother and I have been in hiding right here."

Tromka's jaw slackened. He didn't believe it. "Here?" he said with astonishment. "You've been hiding in Sucha?"

Aron nodded. Tromka realized that they were quite serious.

For seven long, grueling months they lived in various holes in the ground. In these makeshift bunkers, only rats and fear were their constant companions. It sounded like a story too incredible to be believed. Concealing themselves as they did, under the watchful eyes of the German SS High Command, and journeying to places that seemed too bizarre to even contemplate.

Not only had Aron and Abe accomplished this remarkable feat, they *survived.*

Only on this day had they dared walk out openly.

"Do you have any supplies you can spare?" Abe asked Tromka.

The Pole stared at them perplexed and admiring. "I'll get you what I can," he promised. "But listen, both the Russians and the Nazis are still in the region. And the fight is far from finished. We don't know which side will be in charge tomorrow. Control of Sucha has changed hourly. I advise you to remain in hiding for at least another day. This way you'll be able to learn what is going to happen."

They knew that this was sound advice. The Nazis weren't going to give an inch. Tromka provided them with what food he could spare, along with several candles and matches. Abe thanked him, and the brothers returned to the bunker.

This time, though, they felt secure enough not to lock themselves in. With the hatch wide open, they ate and talked excitedly about what they might do after liberation.

Suddenly Aron's heart almost stopped. He heard one of the most terrifying sounds of his life: German soldiers walking directly over their bunker. The small patrol was searching the area for straggling Russians.

Aron promptly extinguished the candles. They held their breath as the Nazis tramped above them. Fortunately, the patrol didn't notice the open hatch, and slowly passed by the bunker and out of sight.

Hearts pounding, Abe and Aron realized that their single moment of carelessness almost cost their lives.

At the very last moment, after such a long struggle for survival, they were almost discovered. If a soldier had seen their light, he would most certainly have lobbed a grenade into the small hole, without caring who might be down there; instant death for the two brothers.

Tromka had been quite right. The Germans were back, probably reinforced. For the moment at least, it was far too early to know who was going to win.

The sound of artillery was soon heard again, and the battle that raged through the night, became more intense than the action of the previous day.

The peace was shattered by fierce bombardments. The sky glowed continually from artillery barrages. Repeatedly the pounding shells destroyed the villages and countryside. Spotter planes moved in and out of the low clouds.

Guarding against any breakthrough, remaining German defenses suffered direct hits. Half-tracks, armored cars, personnel carriers were targets of repeated Russian strikes. The road and fields became littered with smouldering trucks, tanks, large gun emplacements, wrecked anti-aircraft positions. Nazi vehicles negotiated numerous hazardous paths between the bombed equipment. Only to be halted by the massive display of firepower laid down by the tactically mobile Soviet forces.

The killing was staggering. Anti-tank guns were fired in unison. Their roar was formidable. Shielded against return fire by these bursts, Russian engineers, sappers and a number of other troops crossed the main road and established positions. Most were armed with little more than rifles and grenades. However, it did not take very long for them to take advantage of the situation.

Fires were raging all through Sucha and the nearby villages. Farm houses were burning, crumbling from the awesome shell fire. The operation had reached a crucial stage. The Red Army was clearly firing and blasting everything it could to destroy the remaining German fortifications. And now they were succeeding with increasing momentum.

When Soviet units were pinned down in one sector of the road, other units made good progress along secondary routes. Fighting started on all sides. The Nazi defenders were being steadily forced back and separated from their main supply lines. Their strategy and tactics resulted in disorganization and heavy casualties. Any coordination among the hard-pressed German field officers was non-existent. Gradually their situation deteriorated. Urgently needed replacement supplies were not forthcoming. Their supply of ammunition and food was almost entirely depleted. There were no medical supplies. The Red Army had taken full advantage of every breakthrough, every enemy weakness, and successfully fragmented the vital Warsaw-Radom road. Any chance of receiving reinforcements had been nullified.

Nazi positions were savagely dissembled; their dwindling fire-power became no match for the superior ordnance arrayed against them.

Bombardments from effective artillery skillfully concealed continued to blast the roads, and the Soviet commanders were unable to overrun Sucha. The Germans refused to surrender, no matter how badly the situation was for them. Until now they had achieved only minor successes in halting the Soviet forces and regaining lost ground. However they could not continue without reinforcements—and none were forthcoming.

With daring, Soviet soldiers, supported by light artillery, advanced across the burning fields, woods and through the orchard. Assault and machine-gun crews shuttled back and forth along their lines, mowing down many who were in their way. However they still pressed forward, undaunted. The defending Germans were confounded that so little effort was being exerted by the attackers to seek cover. No matter how many fell, twice that amount continued to advance.

A second and third wave of Russians speeded their progress. Mortars and grenades, concentrating on forward positions along the heights, destroyed each German pocket one after another in a brutal killing encounter.

The Nazis displayed tenacity and courage against the onslaught, but their battered command's situation had grown progressively worse and they were unable to repulse the attackers who were now capturing every one of their objectives.

The sheer disparity of numbers started to take its toll; perimeters were shrinking rapidly. SS Headquarters had been severely bombed, and to a man they realized that the Third *Reich*'s days of occupation and rule over Poland and Europe were ended forever.

Well-armed Russians thundered across the blackened encampment, over fences and bodies, barbed wire, and destroyed equipment. Their flanks overran all semblances of resistance. While still perpetuating an elaborate pretense of manning their parameters, German small-fire bursts persisted relentlessly, cutting down as many opposing troops as they could. The Soviets, meanwhile, eliminated defending Germans in small and larger groups. They left behind them grim mementos of failed defenses.

Few prisoners were taken. As position after position was abandoned, lost or blown to smithereens, the Russians methodically shot every enemy soldier they encountered. Those Germans who could still fight, retreated and ran. Some were shot as they headed for the forests, others became victims of the seemingly ceaseless explosions that flattened the tree-studded hills. It was a terrible bloodbath that no surviving participant on either side would soon forget.

Slowly, painstakingly so, the fusillades abated. The fires diminished in number and intensity. The war cries and screams of the dying, gradually came to an end on the thawed ice-battlefield.

The battle for Sucha was over at last.

Chapter Nineteen

The scene was one of devastation. It was the fourteenth of January, 1945. A time and place indelibly etched in Aron's mind. Everywhere were abandoned guns, wreckages of overturned trucks, warped and punctured tanks, skeletal remains of personnel carriers, smoldering farmlands and blackened woodlands.

Dense black smoke hung low beneath the clouds. Fog-like and noxious. Then there were the unnumbered corpses piled high as far as he could see. Many were charred beyond recognition. Grotesque and frightful remains of human beings. The entire landscape was infected with the heavy, sickening odor of death.

Numbed at the magnitude of it all, Aron and Abe could only wander around stunned and amazed.

Rifle-bearing Russians, faces grim and battle-weary, were moving across and over the fields by the hundreds. Fresh troops in quick-step, fleeing one battle and on the way to another.

The grand palace in Sucha was a shambles. Local Poles were busily raiding and stealing whatever they could salvage, clothing, food, kerosene, and various miscellaneous items.

As the brothers wandered in a daze, some of the villagers called out to them. "Hey, come on! Take what you want. The Germans are gone!"

The madness of war had affected everyone, it seemed.

Neither Aron nor Abe would take part in the pillaging. They wanted nothing. Nazi programs and laws had hounded them for years; now it proved to be as valuable as the mounds of rubble the German soldiers left behind. Hitler's agenda for Aryan domination of the world had been smashed like the bones of its staunch adherents. This was the only wish the brothers desired. Now it had been granted to them. Soon it would be fulfilled for everyone.

Shocked, still skeptical about their freedom, they roamed aimlessly, surveying the battle carnage and the desecrating human vultures preying not only on the ruined palace but also on the bodies of the dead; their watches, jewelry, money. It was a shameful sight.

This was the current state of affairs in their world. A world without reason, gone totally insane. Nazi Germany had sowed the seeds. This was their harvest. A bitter macabre harvest indeed.

Trying to gather their thoughts and composure, they started for Janek Koptera's house.

A broad smile greeted them. Triumph made his face glow; victory over the killers at last.

Koptera embraced them, saying, "See, I told you that you'd survive. Thank God, at least for us, this war is over."

189

He led them into the cottage, and quickly brought out the things Abe had left in his charge. Pleased, he handed them the faded photographs and the gold coins.

"I will give thanks in church for the miracle of your survival," he said. Justice had conquered criminality. "May you find other members of your family alive and well."

Abe thanked him for his valuable help, and they left.

Along the road, not far from the charred wreckage, they met a middle-aged Polish woman with whom Abe had once worked in Sucha's kitchens. She, too, was astonished at finding the young brothers alive.

"Why didn't you come to me if you needed help?" she chastised them. "I would have done what I could for you."

Inside Aron and Abe laughed at her belated offer of assistance. Now that the war was over it seemed that everyone was their friend again. They all insisted that they would have offered support and sustenance.

Next, they went to visit the mill's manager, Tromka. He invited them inside his tidy small home and served them hot tea and biscuits. They talked for a long time about many things. Tromka seemed genuinely surprised when Abe confessed that it had been he and Aron who broke into his mill, smashed the windows and stole his sacks of flour.

Tromka's eyes widened. "Then it was you two who took the tools and brought them to the edge of the woods?"

"It was," admitted Aron. "We were building a new bunker for ourselves. We were working in the bitter cold when a soldier quite accidently came by and surprised us."

The mill manager could not believe what he was

hearing. "Do you know who that soldier was?" he asked incredulously. Answering his own question, he went on, "That man was a doctor who'd been assigned to Sucha. A German physician who'd been staying with me in this very house."

Aron and Abe shared glances.

"And I'll tell you what else," added Tromka vigorously. "When this German doctor returned to my house for his breakfast, after his walk, he told me how he had spotted two youths at the forest's edge. He saw that you were unarmed, and he just couldn't bring himself to shoot you. He knew that in allowing you to escape he was committing a crime against the *Reich*, but he still couldn't do it."

It was a lonely walk back to the village of their birth; Bialobrzegi. It had been that long. At the home of their neighbor they washed and changed their clothes. They were very dirty indeed; holed up for seven months in their bunker, wearing the same shirts.

They ate a hot meal, then slept. On the following morning they took a walk on the town's main street. Because the war had ended, the townsfolk in this sector were in a gala mood, ready for celebrating. They started to sing, dance, and drink vodka in the square.

But Aron and Abe did not imbibe, nor did they dance. Rather, they stood tearfully, mourning their murdered family. It appeared that no one survived; no friends, no relatives. They wondered, if perhaps, they were the only two Jewish survivors in all of Poland.

They continued roving through the town. Nazi corpses were strewn everywhere: In the streets, in the alleys, and especially on the road. No one bothered to collect the bodies. Civilians spat on them, as they passed.

As Aron and Abe took another path away from this nightmare of the dead they were recognized and greeted by various townspeople who remembered them. Old schoolmates from earlier days, tradesmen from the markets, and laborers. They all seemed pleased and imbued with goodwill for their Jewish brothers, welcoming them back, sorrowfully, recounting the horrible things that had taken place during those unbearable years of intolerable occupation.

Their courtesy was accepted, but it rang hollow.

Soon, however, they met another face from the past. The man approached them staring with squinting eyes.

"My God," cried Aron as he returned the stare. "It's Meyer Szerman." Another Jew; another one of us was alive!

"How did you manage to live through this ordeal?" Meyer asked them after a genuinely emotional greeting.

Aron related their long, painful story.

Meyer was equally astonished at their tenacity; their courage to have lived through so many trials. Smiling, he finally said, "Quite a few other members of your family are still alive, you know."

Aron was in shock. "What, our family alive? Are you sure, Meyer?"

"Yes, I'm certain. They are in a village not seven kilometers from here. I know because I stayed in hiding with them. There was a Polish family named Kuroska who cared for us all. Gave us a place to hide . . ."

The brothers didn't know what to say.

Meyer laughed. "It's true, I tell you. Come with me. Your cousins and uncles are waiting."

Mrs. Kuroska was an exceptional woman by any standards; placing her life in terrible jeopardy, she safely hid eleven people. Eleven Jews who were spared from the Treblinka gas chambers because of her remarkable courage.

She had been a lifelong friend of Mama, Aron recalled, and after their escape from Pionki they would gladly have asked her for help but none of them knew where she was living.

It was one day after they were liberated that they came to her village and house. She looked at them with expressively joyful eyes. "Come inside, both of you," she said. She kissed and hugged them again and again. Then, sternly like a mother, she demanded that they take off what they were wearing and throw those filthy rags away. Like caring for infants she helped to wash them with warm water in the tub. It was difficult to wash away all the dirt, grime and filth that had accumulated. When their baths were over, she provided them with fresh clothes and fed them.

This gentle, kind Christian, Mrs. Kuroska, had provided refuge to two of Mama's brothers as well as her sisters, and several of their friends as well. Aron and Abe spent some time with her, and with their family, reacquainting themselves with loved ones they never expected to see again.

They listened incredulously as the stories were recounted of Jews who were sent to the notorious death camps, ordered to take off their clothes so they could shower, and then, packed together by the hundreds, were put to death as poison gas—not water—came out of the showers. Women, children, the elderly and feeble, along with the men. There were no exceptions. Afterwards, the bodies were hauled away to the waiting ovens, and cremated.

The Nazis had studiously developed their inhuman instruments into a deadly science. Hour after hour, new groups were delivered and slaughtered. The trains arrived at the camps twenty-four hours a day, seven days a week. During the last year, when it became apparent that the war was lost, the Nazis intensified their slaughter of Jews. It was merely a matter of logistics to them. First bringing the Jews to the trains. Then determining how many of them could be herded into a single train, and how many could be killed and cremated in a single day. Lastly, accelerating their efforts to hurry the killings while there was still time—they thought—to annihilate the entire Jewish people.

Aron was repulsed and sickened. The worst fears he had in Pionki had all been verified, quite accurate. He tried not to picture Papa or any of his family suffering such an awful death. It was all incomprehensible.

Soon after, they were ready to return to Bialobrzegi. They said their fond farewells to their relatives and to dear Mrs. Kuroska.

"I have something for you to take back," she announced as they started to leave.

"We really don't need anything."

She brushed the refusal aside with a gesture of her hand, unwilling to hear of it. "What I have for you will be quite useful, believe me. It's a surprise."

The surprise was a sewing machine: Abe had been trained as a tailor, and as soon as they returned to their home he set up shop, and made pants and jackets for the people of the town.

A great deal of freedom was allowed by the Russians during the last months of the war, but it soon became apparent that the communists had come to Poland to stay. Their own political philosophy was to be the new order. Local Polish party members were already being given high posts.

Aron also found work as a glass cutter, repairing

some of the widespread damage. It was a vast undertaking; hardly a window anywhere was left intact during the severe fighting.

The local civil service Poles who were under the jurisdiction of the Soviet authorities, found the brothers a room. It was small, but clean. They could come and go as they pleased. Such freedom felt strange after so many years of imprisonment.

Gradually, as the weeks passed, a few more of their old friends made their way back to the scenic, but unimportant little town. Before the war, Bialobrzegi had been home to some four hundred Jewish families, almost half of the total population.

After liberation, the number of Jewish survivors was reduced to a total of sixty five.

Part Four

Chapter Twenty

During 1945, the war was still raging despite the liberation of Poland by the Red Army. The wanton killing of Jews did not cease. Aron received word that in Radom one of his cousins had been murdered after he returned to search for survivors in his family. It was reported that the Poles who committed this crime did so because they were afraid that he would try and reclaim his house. The brutality of this atrocity disgusted Aron.

How could such a mindless crime happen? Poland was free of its Nazi overlords. It was a grim reminder for him, of just how precarious the lives of those remaining Jews rea,ly were.

This was what became of his war-torn nation after years of frightful occupation. Was it all a land of savages and scavengers? bereft of even a modicum of human decency, little better than the Nazis?

However, even under these stresses and abominations, life still had to continue. And through this period Aron found himself thinking more and more about the fate of Jacob. Was his brother still alive, too? If so, why hadn't anyone heard about him? Or did the Russians prevent him from returning to his family?

Although he didn't know it then, this unanswered question would persist for years to come.

Aron and Abe soon moved into a house with five of their friends. All of them were working now, trying their best to lead normal lives. Normalcy, however, was a goal that the surviving Jews of Poland—and all of Europe—would find difficult to attain.

They ate regular meals for the first time, and gradually regained their health. As the pain and sorrow diminished they even found renewed hope for the future.

Aron, though, continued to brood. The death of his cousin in Radom affected him seriously. The bitter memories would not leave. He was haunted by them. After much discussion with his brother, he decided it would be better for him if he left Bialbrzegi to start a new life elsewhere.

He arrived in the city of Lodz along with his friend Meyer Seigelman. Abe, it had been agreed, would join them there shortly.

During these weeks Berlin was under siege. Russian troops were constantly being ferried back and forth from Poland to the new and last front: the assault on Germany's capital.

The train transporting soldiers took them near Lodz. Aron and Meyer found that the Soviet troops were in dire need of warm clothing. The hastily retreating Germans had left many such supplies behind, scattered about in the billeted homes of the Nazi troops. The youths gathered as many useful items as they could find, and sold them on the train as it stopped.

Abe and another friend, Velvo, came to Lodz, and joined them in this venture. The poorly-clad Russian troops were eager to buy whatever clothing was available, and the money they received allowed them to carry on under the harsh conditions imposed on the strife-ridden country.

The four pooled their resources. Whatever meager funds were earned went into a single repository. They cooked meals for one another, always ate together, and even made clothes for themselves whenever necessary. Occasionally, when other friends arrived in Lodz, they became the beneficiaries of their hospitality.

The reports in the newspapers and on the radio were now sanguine: World War II was coming to an end.

By mid April of 1945, the Red Army had launched its big push: the battle to capture Berlin, the very heart of the Third *Reich*.

Marshal Zhukov's First Belorussian Front and Marshal Koniev's First Ukrainian Front began their great offensives. More than two and one half million soldiers, supported by commensurate battalions of aircraft, artillery and tanks, attacked the beleaguered city in force. On the twenty fifth of April units from both these armies linked up, completing the encirclement of the besieged city. The Soviet stranglehold on the capital could not be broken.

The fierce battle developed into a painfully slow struggle; street by street the fighting was being waged. The clash ranked among the bloodiest of the entire war. Germany was now brought to its knees, with the vengeful Soviets the victor.

The date was April 30, 1945. *Reichführer* Hitler committed suicide in his own bunker deep beneath the *Reich*'s Chancellery.

When the final battle was over, on May second, German Lt. General Weidling formally surrendered both Berlin and its half-million defenders to the Russians.

Red Army casualties during the siege of Berlin numbered some three hundred thousand. The German losses were even more staggering: over one million.

On May 8, in the capital, the victorious Russians staged a flamboyant surrender ceremony that equaled the one staged by the Western Allies on the previous day in Reims, France.

At long last, in Europe, World War II was over.

All through the world, it was a time of joy. For Aron and Abe it was a time for prayer. God had been good to them; they survived.

Almost six months after liberation Aron received by mail, unexpected official papers from the Polish government.

"What have you got there?" Abe asked with curiosity.

Aron showed him the document in utter disbelief. "I have been instructed to report for duty in the Polish Army. Drafted for three years to fight for Poland."

Abe asked seriously, "What are you going to do?"

Aron laughed after he read the official notice. "After being a prisoner in a concentration camp, then a fugitive on the run from both the Nazis and the Polish partisans, do you really think I'm going to serve in Poland's new army? Fighting for *them*?" The very idea seemed ridiculous.

No, he'd had his belly full of Poland. Itzhak's senseless death at the hands of AK partisans had left no doubt regarding most Poles' feelings about its remaining Jews. They were not welcome; it was that simple. Nor did Aron himself desire to remain a part of their bloodstained land. Before the war, in 1939, there were well over three million Jews in Poland. Almost one tenth of the entire population. Three million of them had been murdered; only several hundred thousand had survived what had come to be known as the Holocaust, and very few of these showed any desire to remain.

The time for Aron had come. He would be leaving the country of his birth; leaving Poland forever.

The American operated camps for displaced persons were located inside defeated Germany. Once one was admitted to a DP camp there was a good possibility of being permitted to emigrate from Europe. Some of the survivors went to Canada, a number, to Australia. Most, though, preferred America or Israel. It was with these possible destinations in mind, that Aron departed for Germany.

Aron, along with his friend Meyer, and his wife, boarded the train to the city of Scziecin. From there they hitchhiked to Berlin. Standing along the busy road they raised their arms, holding salamis and bottles of vodka. In a little while a truck carrying Russian soldiers stopped and picked them up.

It was about midnight when they reached the German capital. The city had been destroyed. No longer a city, only the rubble of what once had been. Street after street, neighborhood after neighborhood. *Berlin Mitte, Penzlauer Berg, Friedrichshain,* all districts of renown, were now totally razed. The New West End, what was soon to be called West Berlin, was gone. Blown away, smashed and crushed. Heaping piles of bricks and wood, empty shells and pitiful remains, like grim desolate creatures clinging ignominiously. The wreckage was total. The Soviets had seen to that. Hardly a building was left standing anywhere, and even those few that did remain bore the unmistakeable scars of war. Daily Allied bombings and the resulting fires had transformed this once great city of culture and science into a mass of ruins. A world of chaos. Tens of thousands dead. Hundreds of thousands wounded and starving. A terrible place, of forlorn and sickly-looking women foraging through the debris. A hell on earth.

As Aron and his two companions walked these gutted streets he didn't feel the pity normally reserved for fellow human beings. In his rage, his hatred for those who savaged the Jewish people, he could think only that these survivors in Berlin had received no less than they deserved. Hitler's Third Reich had been responsible not only for the deaths of six million Jews, but of twenty million Russians, hundreds of thousands of freedom-loving Poles, French, Dutch, Czechs, and many millions of other innocent Europeans. Yes, and even the deaths of thousands of other Germans, those who bravely stood up and protested openly against Nazi fascism. Socialists, intellectuals, writers, artists, jurists, liberals, communists, journalists, democrats, ministers, priests of every background and ideology. The elite of its own society. The list of victims was endless. If Germany had suffered, then it was a small price to pay for the grievous tortures of others it had so wrongfully committed.

They kept in the darkness and among the ruins. In the distance they saw a light from behind the window of a still standing house. Because almost every structure had been razed, it seemed that this house was close, so they headed towards it, hoping to find a place to sleep. It turned into a very long walk.

When they finally reached it, they found only half a house standing. Aron knocked on the door. "Please open up," he said. "We're looking for a place to sleep. We won't harm anyone. We have food we can give you."

A frail woman with deep wrinkles and stringy hair opened the door slightly. "I hope you're telling me the truth," she said. Then she allowed the three strangers to enter.

She lived there with her daughter, she told them. She confided to her unexpected guests that she was too frightened to venture outside because of the presence of Russian soldiers all over the city. Rape and/or mass murder was what they might expect. Thus, neither she nor her daughter had eaten anything for days.

Aron and Meyer gave them food. The irony of Jews now feeding Germans was not lost on them.

The woman took what they gave gratefully, then offered her guests a place to sleep. A dark corner of a chilly room. On the next day Aron and his group were admitted into an American DP camp.

The Americans were extremely kind. They welcomed the refugees, and served them meals, beds and medical treatment. Within a single month Aron's health had returned. He could look into a mirror and like what he saw; a man, a human being.

This divided city, however, was not where Aron wanted to stay. He yearned to feel free, to live among other Jews, and perhaps find a place for himself in America.

He remained restless. A young man in search of himself. He left the DP camp with some sadness, and went back on the road. First to Munich, then Feldafing, finally to Frankfurt. There he was joined by Abe.

He had many sleepless nights, disturbed by bad dreams, he relived the continuing nightmare of the past six years.

Indelibly etched in his heart and soul was the memory of his family. Brucha, Ester. Simon, Itzhak. And most of all there was Papa. So often, when he sat quietly alone, he could see Papa standing before him. He would remember those final, but prophetic words:

Go, my son. Maybe you will survive. . . .

In time Aron and Abe settled in a new DP camp in Lambartim, where there were a thousand Jewish families. With an uncle and a cousin, they moved into a nice villa. Abe took a job as a security policeman for the camp. Aron decided not to seek any steady job. Instead, he travelled from town to town, and to cities, buying and selling food. During the four years that were to pass, he earned a good living. The young shoemaker, as it turned out, was quite a good businessman.

He had many friends. Usually, they would all meet at a favorite local restaurant everyday for breakfast, lunch, and dinner. Only Aron had enough money to pay; and he did so for all his friends. He was a leader, and they followed him. Making money was not a problem, and he would often tell his friends, "Whatever I have, can be yours as well.

The black market was conducting a thriving business. Aron's little venture soon found him involved in buying and selling gold, fine watches, and just about anything that was available. His customers included Russians, Ukrainians, and all kinds of people.

Things went well—mostly.

"I have a lot of goods for you, Aron," a black marketeer informed him. It was a man with whom Aron had dealings previously, so he believed that he could trust him.

"I want you to meet me in Manheim," the trader said. "If you can bring me seven or eight hundred American dollars I can make a lot of money for you."

Aron agreed. He gathered every penny he could

raise and with some five hundred dollars in his pocket he left for Manheim, about thirty kilometers away. He also agreed to tell no one—not even Abe—where he was going.

They had arranged to meet in an empty building for the transaction. Of course, Aron came alone. The black marketeer appeared with a number of his friends.

"Did you bring the money?"

"I have it," replied Aron.

"Good."

The man smiled. "Then raise your hands—and give me everything you have."

One of the friends aimed a gun at him.

Aron realized that he had no alternative but to comply. They stole everything. They fled, leaving Aron there alone, with empty pockets. He did not even have enough money to get back to the camp.

Angry at himself, depressed by this sudden sour turn of events, he sought out a fellow he knew named Stone. This man drove a truck fueled by wood. He had done some business with young Aron in the past and liked him very much. Dejectedly, Aron came to his house.

After Stone's wife and two children left the room, Aron told him what had happened.

"Stone, I have no money. The way you see me now, that's all I own. Nothing's left. Nothing."

Stone drove Aron all the way back to Lambartim, and gave his young friend some money.

"I'll pay this back—with interest," he said as he got out of the truck.

Stone shook his head. "No, Aron. I don't need the money. Just be careful, alright?" and he drove off.

Aron walked quietly into the villa and went to his room. He didn't dare tell his brother or his uncle what had happened, what a fool he had been to trust people in the black market. He decided to speak with a highly successful businessman he knew named Pelta Friedman.

"Don't tell my family, please, Pelta, but I've just been robbed. Everything's gone."

Pelta was shocked. "Are you all right?"

Aron nodded. Except for his wounded pride he was fine.

"What can I do for you?"

"Lend me fifty dollars."

Pelta handed him the money. Before Aron could say anything, Pelta said, "Don't worry, I know you'll find some way to make it all back."

It had been a painful lesson, but one that had taught him much.

In the city of Frankfurt lived a mutual friend of his and Pelta's, 'Maniac' Glina. Also a black market trader, and a highly successful one at that, he was much older than Aron, but had taken a liking to the hard-working youth.

A few days after the Manheim incident Aron was standing with his friends outside of their favorite restaurant. Just then a dark, gleaming, polished limousine pulled up directly in front of them. It was a brand new auto called an *Opel Capitain.*

A well-dressed chauffeur opened the car's back door, and Maniac Glina slowly stepped out. He brushed some lint from his jacket, toyed with his expensive cufflinks, and looked at the group outside of the restaurant. He was a man of some repute.

Maniac walked over to Aron, greeted him with a hearty handshake, and said, "I want you to come with me."

"Where do you want me to go?"

"Let's you and I have some dinner, all right?"

"I can't leave my friends here," Aron protested, pointing to the small group behind him. "We all came together."

Maniac seemed determined. "It'll only take few moments. I want to speak with you. Why don't we have a drink and something to eat?"

Half-heartedly, Aron agreed. Maniac Glina had something in mind, he was sure.

Maniac also knew that his young friend was without funds, but as they entered the restaurant, he said, "You're going to pay for our supper tonight."

Aron swallowed hard. "Fine with me," he said. Although he had no money at all, he knew that his credit was good at the eatery.

Maniac ordered his dinner, and sat there eating, drinking and savoring every bite. Suddenly he looked up at his puzzled companion and said, "You know something, Aron, I'm angry with you. Yes. Very angry."

"With me? Why? What wrong have I done you?"

Maniac smiled slyly. "I had to learn from Pelta that you're broke? That you were robbed and have no money?" He leaned across the table, closer to Aron. "You know that I'm your friend, don't you?"

"Of course I know that," said a surprised Aron. "You've been a good friend all the way. But I couldn't bring myself to ask you for anything."

"If someone is a friend then you don't have to be embarrassed, do you?" Maniac admonished him. Then without another word he reached deep into the pocket of his trousers and pulled out a wad of bills. He counted one thousand American dollars in cash, and handed it to the startled young man, saying, "I want you to take it."

"Maniac, listen to me. If I lose this money, if any-thing unforeseen should happen, I won't be able to pay you back. . . ."

"Aron, if you lose it, don't worry about it, all right?"

"Look, Maniac. If this money were mine, then all right, I'm not afraid. I wouldn't care. But to be re-sponsible for somebody else's cash?—No, I'm too afraid of losing it."

Maniac sighed deeply, and turned his head. "See that car there?" He pointed to his waiting limo. "Tomorrow morning this limousine will be waiting right in front of your house. I want you to take a ride with my chauffeur to Berlin. Let's say it's a trip to see some of my friends. They're waiting for me. I've hidden black market dollars in several places inside the car. You'll have to pass Russian checkpoints and border guards, understand? They won't find anything, not the way I've hidden things." He smiled. "Then you're going to convert the dollars and bring back German marks, got all that straight? Don't be frightened. It's done all the time, and the border guards won't know where to find the money. Will you do this for me? Can I count on you?"

Aron agreed to do exactly as Maniac had asked.

The next day the car was waiting for him outside his home. They arrived in Berlin, met clandestinely with Maniac's connections, and quickly exchanged the cur-rency. Then they returned safe and sound, precisely as Maniac had predicted they would.

Aron came out of the affair with a huge profit to show for his time and trouble. Easy money, Maniac had assured him. Aron reluctantly agreed to make the same trip several times more.

As soon as he was able, he paid Maniac back all the

money he borrowed and still found himself with quite a substantial amount of cash left over.

Soon after, he met with Maniac Glina and told him that he'd had enough.

"Why? Don't you believe this can make you a very rich man?" asked Maniac.

"Maybe. But this is dangerous work; extremely so, and I don't plan to spend the rest of my life in an American or Russian prison."

Chapter Twenty One

By 1948 life had become quite pleasant. Aron had become a well-respected, and firmly-established resident of the DP camp known as Lambartim. He got to knowing the right people, and how to make things happen.

There was a cinema in the camp that he used to frequent. One night there was a long line waiting to see the film version of Victor Hugo's *The Hunchback of Notre Dame*. Tickets were very difficult to come by unless you had connections, and Aron had them.

As he walked past the waiting line, he noticed the comely figure of a pretty young woman waiting with a group of friends, hoping to obtain tickets. He had seen her before on occasion, and remembered that her name was Ester. She had come to the camp with about fifty other families who escaped from Poland and went to the Soviet Union. She was about seventeen, with lovely long blond hair, and seemed shy. As Aron stood outside the theater he kept his eye on her.

Taking a deep breath, summoning all his courage, he approached her. "You want to get a ticket for the film?" he asked.

She nodded. Her eyes were bright and limpid. She had a charming smile that he found irresistible.

"Good. I can get you a ticket."

Ester Disman raised a slender hand. Her long, shiny hair bounced off her shoulders. "But I can't go without my friend, Nahamma. Can you get her a ticket, too?"

Aron tried not to frown. Ester, he was soon to learn, never went anywhere without Nahamma Fisher. If he wanted to take Ester out, he was going to have to include Nahamma. It was as simple as that.

"Alright," he said. "I think I can get us three tickets."

That evening, Aron, Ester, and Nahamma went to the movies.

He courted Ester regularly, meeting her parents, Rachel and Josef, and got to know her three other younger sisters, Rivka, who was the eldest of the rest, followed by Miriam who was only two, and young Sara, who was not quite one year old. He liked the entire Disman family immediately, and became a frequent visitor to their humble home.

Love bloomed for Aron for the first time in his life. Thinking back, he never believed that he would ever be ready to start a family of his own. That day, however, would be coming quite soon.

On February 20, 1949, Aron Goldfarb and Ester Disman were married.

The State of Israel was formed and recognized some nine months earlier. After fighting a difficult war against all of its Arab neighbors, the 650,000 Jews of the British Mandate of Palestine founded the free and independent state of Israel. A country that was to be the homeland of all the Jews throughout the world.

The land of the Bible, of Moses, and of the Hebrew tribes.

At last, after almost two thousand years of exile and persecution, the Jews had a nation of their own. One of the first acts enacted by the infant state was the Law of Return. Any Jew, not only in Europe, but in any country in the world, was invited to settle and help build a new and modern nation.

Aron had never been an ardent Zionist, but he always dreamed of living as a free man in a country of his own people. In July of 1949, amid hardship and constant undeclared war, Aron and his new bride left the DP camp and emigrated to Israel.

Life proved to be very difficult for them indeed. The influx of survivors into the small nation resulted in a drastic shortage of housing and jobs. The new arrivals were hurriedly and temporarily placed in cities of tents.

Everyone struggled, and Aron was no exception. It was a harsh, and largely arid land, with temperatures soaring to heat most Europeans had never experienced. Desert and semi-Desert lands were places they only read about in books. Now they were finding out what it was actually like.

Nevertheless, they all remained content. They were safe from the hardships and terrors of the past, and they were now an integral part of a new bustling nation they proudly called their own. Aron and Ester were very happy.

Soon one other event made Aron even happier.

In 1950, Jacob Goldfarb at last came home.

He had returned to his family ten years after fleeing to the Soviet Union for safety. Half of that time had been spent in a Russian prison camp in Siberia.

It had been an emotional experience for Aron, indeed for all of them, that day when they met for the first time after such a long interval. Aron had been anxiously waiting for his arrival for days in the port city of Haifa, Israel. Since Jacob had been a citizen of Poland, the Soviets released and returned him to that country. Since his wife and children were safe and waiting for him in Breslaw, Aron and Abe kept in touch with them since the end of the war. Thus, Jacob knew where to find his brothers.

He seemed older, more subdued; he sat back in the comfortable chair, Aron was seated with his family on either side, and they listened attentively as he related what had happened to him during his long absence.

During 1940 he was a laborer for the Germans, much as Abe and Itzhak had been. One day he was unfairly accused of stealing something from an office. Jacob protested his innocence to the authorities. They refused to listen to anything he had to say. Jacob Goldfarb was a Jew, and so the petty theft was immediately blamed on him without even an investigation.

The Nazi occupation of Poland was still recent at that time, and it was still possible for anyone to slip or be smuggled out of the country. He knew that this was to be his only recourse.

He fled, eastward, crossing into Soviet territory. Their greeting was not what he had expected.

The Russians accepted him and quickly put him to work for their war effort. Jacob toiled for them during all of the difficult years of the war. In 1945, he was working as a foreman in a Moscow factory that manufactured coats for the Red Army. One of his duties was ordering supplies. The Soviet system was difficult at best—and sometimes impossible.

On one particular occasion he requested needles to complete an order of garments. Instead of needles he received more lining. The next time he ordered lining he was sent a now unneeded supply of needles.

"What's going on here?" Jacob justly complained to his superiors. "I'm trying to keep everyone working. If I ask for needles, I must have needles. Otherwise I can't fill the quota."

Challenging the bureaucracy was dangerous. The Soviets had little sympathy for someone who was always questioning the way things were being done.

Orders from above filtered down. Jacob Goldfarb was to be arrested and charged as a German spy, trying to stir up discontent among the workers and organizing them against the government.

The idea of a Jew, working secretly for the Nazis was ridiculous to say the least.

That did not matter to his superiors, however. He was found guilty as charged.

Sent to a labor camp in Siberia, he was beaten quite often by the military police. He would be roused in the middle of the night, and tortured, time and again.

The situation was grimly reminiscent of the scenes in Orwell's famous book, *1984*.

"See that wall in front of you, Goldfarb?" they would taunt him.

Bloodied, he would nod that he did.

"What color is it?"

"White."

The wall indeed was white, but they would continue to beat him, saying, "If we tell you it's black, then you're going to swear that it's black."

That was his fate under the harsh realities of Stalin's dictatorship. Five years in prison, because he had tried to do the right thing.

A few months later Aron received papers ordering him to report for obligatory military service in the newly created IDF, Israel Defense Force. Ester was pregnant with their first child. She cried when she received the news. Aron was distressed. He had no objection to serving in the army of his country, but who would remain to care for his wife and as yet unborn child during his long absence? He worried for a long time over the matter. There was, however, a solution to the problem.

There was only one way to avoid military service. In an effort to cultivate the barren land, the Government decreed that anyone willing to farm would be exempted from the thirty months of mandatory service.

Aron and Ester discussed the matter through the long, worrisome night.

"I don't know anything about farming, and neither do you," she protested.

He shrugged. "Unless you're prepared for my absence for two and a half years, we have no choice."

He knew that realistically Ester's position was correct. He knew absolutely nothing about farming. His father and no one in his family had ever done any farming. What did he know about milking cows, planting crops, and harvesting? As little as he knew about agriculture, Ester knew even less. The whole plan seemed absurd. Nevertheless, he tried to convince his wife that moving to a farm was the best thing for them. Convincing her was not going to be easy. She loathed the idea.

"All right then, why don't you decide," he said, in exasperation.

"Me, decide?" Ester was flustered.

Aron looked at her sternly. "Do you want me to leave as a soldier or remain with you as a farmer?"

The choices were not very appealing.

Thus it was that Aron became a homesteader. The government leased the land to them. They settled in a

217

village called *Kfar Warburg*, which was named for a wealthy American philanthropic family. Aron became a farmer of sorts, and periodically served in the military reserve.

Shortly after they settled down, their first child was born. Aron prayed for a son during all of Ester's pregnancy. A child to name after Papa.

When Ester finally went into labor her mother remained with her throughout the night in the local hospital. Rachel Disman came to her son-in-law the following morning with a wide smile on her face. His prayers had been answered.

On September 13, 1951, the first day of the High Holy Days, Aron became the proud father of a son.

There was no question as to what his name would be. They called him Morris, after Moshe, his father. He thought of how proud Papa would have been to see his grandson. Tears welled up Aron's blue eyes, and he recalled the pain and suffering of the war. It was the most joyous day of his young life. Not only had he survived, but through his child Papa's heritage would continue.

There were some thirty eight families in the farming commune. They worked, ate, and spent their free time together. Despite the heat and the hard work, they were a happy group. All refugees, all survivors of the terrible Holocaust, together, sharing a part of their new homeland, Israel. They could not have been more delighted.

Yes, they were free—but they were not safe. Their village was dangerously close to the borders of hostile Jordan. Each night they took turns guarding the parameters of their territory. Arab incursions and killings were all too frequent. On every third day Aron, with a pistol strapped to his belt, and a rifle slung over his shoulder, served as a guard to protect not only their farms, but the very borders of the State of Israel.

During the days, the village men became construction workers, building their own homes and those of their neighbors. Government specialists taught them how to make bricks, lay foundations, and install plumbing. The indefatigable citizens would work on ten homes at a time. When those were finished they would start ten more. Within the short span of eight months, the entire community was completely built. There were no luxuries; fresh water and plumbing were outside of the houses. But these were their homes, erected by themselves, and they were very proud of them. During the construction of their homes, the government subsidized the farmers for their basic needs.

As hard as Aron worked, though, and as many hours as he toiled, he could not earn a living from his farming. So he took a second job. Each morning he would rise at four and join several of his friends on a job of unloading milk containers. They would remove them from a freezer, load them on trucks that were driven to Israel's largest city, Tel Aviv. Depending on the number of cartons to be loaded for the day, they usually finished their work at dawn. During those few hours a day Aron earned as much money as many of the others did on their regular jobs. Loading was difficult and unpopular work, so those who performed this task were relatively well paid. He was young and strong and didn't object to the hard labor. All he wanted was to provide a good living for his small family.

After toiling all day on the farm, he took yet a third job at night. At about seven, a number of trailers from Tel Aviv would arrive, loaded with sacks of pesticides for the fields. With three others, Aron would climb a ladder, lift the sacks onto his back, and unload them. It would often take long hours to unload the heavy chemical-filled sacks, and although Aron never looked at his watch he knew that sometimes he worked as much as twenty hours a day.

It didn't matter. His reward was the smile on his son's face, the happiness in his eyes. That was more than ample compensation.

One day, Jacob came and watched them working. When the unloading finished he approached Aron with tears in the corners of his eyes. "I can't stand to see you toiling like this," he said. "My heart is crying for you."

Aron regarded his brother with a smile. "Jacob, for me, nothing is too difficult. I'm in my own country, and for the first time ever I really feel good."

Chickens and turkeys often scampered freely about the farm. While the young children were at school, the mothers helped with the seemingly endless, tedious work. Ester found herself helping in the vegetable garden; planting and caring for the tomatoes, cucumbers, onions, and the like. They all labored seven days a week. A farmer, as Aron learned, rarely gets even a single day off.

Even though life was difficult, there were times for enjoyment. Some evenings they would travel to Tel Aviv to go to the theater or an opera. At other times they would be content to go to the nearest cinema. This became a therapeutic respite from the daily drudgery.

The government provided each farming family with one cow, three months pregnant. Since there was no barn for the animal, one had to be built. In the meantime, each of the cows remained tethered to a post outside the house.

Aron's own cow proved to be a particularly troublesome one. She was unaptly named *Chedva*, or 'Happy'.

Aron was not easily frightened after all he'd been through, but he dared not go near this bovine animal. Whenever he tried to feed or water the beast she would kick wildly at him, or butt him like a bull with her huge head. Aron would drop her food quickly, even toss it to her, and then run for his life.

Chedva finally gave birth.

A number of the village people knew about grooming and milking, but not Aron. He had no idea at all about what to do. But his cow was now a mother, and she had to be milked.

Aron reluctantly spoke with a neighbor. "My friend," he said, "maybe you can help me. I don't know how to milk this cow. And Ester—forget it."

"Don't worry, Aron," answered the man, who used to be a carpenter. "Come with me and I'll show you how it's done."

Aron shrugged and followed.

The neighbor approached the cow and sat on a stool. With his left hand he held her legs, and with his right he began to tug at her teats, and milked her. Then he turned to Aron. "Now you sit and try it."

"But I can't. I still don't know how . . ."

"Just sit down and pull, as I was doing."

Bravely, Aron replaced his neighbor on the stool. He did as he was shown, and to his amazement he milked her. First one bucket, then another.

He scratched his head. "I don't know, something isn't right with this cow of mine."

"Never mind," replied the neighbor, offering yet another bucket. "She's probably one of the best, that's why she's giving so much milk."

A few days later, the barn was finished. He took her inside and tethered her. From that day on *Chedva* wouldn't let anybody near her except Aron. There were no longer any problems with her. She didn't kick or carry on, and in fact she gave so much milk that envious professional farmers would come to see, and marvel.

"It's just not normal," they would mutter as they left. Aron laughed.

While he was away on reserve duty his mother-in-law, Rachel, tried to help out by milking *Chedva.* The cow went berserk, pushed her against the wall, and almost killed the woman.

Young Morris was about six months old. Aron and Ester dutifully went about their business, improving their small farm. Soon Aron was blessed with seven milking cows and five calves. They were also the proud owners of a horse. Actually it wasn't a regular horse, but a cross between a horse and a donkey.

The horse also proved to be a problem. For some inexplicable reason he didn't like to leave the village. Every time Aron tried to take him out, the animal would resist, turn around half a dozen times, and snort.

One particular Saturday their next door neighbor, Meyer Landow, had a birthday party for his young son. All the villagers were invited, including Aron and his family.

"I'll be a little late," Aron informed them. "I have something to do before I go."

It was a chore he never liked; feeding the horse. Food in a bucket, Aron knelt to give it to him. The horse kicked swiftly and hit Aron in the chest with such a power that Aron was knocked unconscious. He lay on the floor for about fifteen minutes, while Ester and their neighbor went to look for him.

When Aron regained his senses, he rose, brushed himself off, and appeared at the birthday party. He explained the reason for his tardiness and apologized.

He decided to teach this recalcitrant animal a lesson once and for all. After all the grief he had suffered during his lifetime he was determined that no one or nothing was ever going to take advantage of him again. Not even this damned horse, *especially.*

He went to the yard, harnessed the animal, and hitched him to a wagon constructed of very heavy metal. Then he placed pieces of wood between the wheels so the wagon would be even harder to pull. Aron then took him out to a recently plowed field. For three quarters of an hour he drove that weary animal back and forth over the field.

The horse was exhausted. Satisfied, Aron returned home with the animal. After that harrowing experience the equine never misbehaved again. Each time Aron would pass, the horse would stand motionless.

When it was time to return for his stint in the army reserve, Aron was told to report to the military base Bedjubrine. The camp skirted the Jordanian border. Several of Aron's friends had been killed while on duty in that area, shot by Jordanian snipers hiding in the hills. It was considered a high risk tour of duty.

After two weeks of arduous patrolling, Aron decided to speak with his commanding officer.

He saluted and stood at attention. The officer looked up at him. "Yes, Private?"

"Sir," he began, "I have a wife and small baby back home on my farm. I am respectfully requesting a weekend pass to go home and be with them. My wife is alone, and she can't manage the farm by herself. I'm asking for leave until either Sunday night, or Monday morning."

The captain listened with interest. He then asked

Aron a few questions about where he had come from, and how he arrived in Israel. Aron in response told him a little about his life.

"All right, soldier," said the officer at length. "Request granted. You'll be on leave until Monday morning. That's all."

Aron saluted and turned smartly about. He was beaming with joy.

When a soldier returns from duty he brings his weapons home with him. This was a standard Israeli practice and regulation. With so many enemies and so many miles of open frontier to protect, a reservist might be called up again at any time, even during the middle of the night. Reserve soldiers have to be on call wherever they are, twenty-four hours a day, seven days a week.

The base was situated only five kilometers from the main road, which started from the Negev town of Beersheva, close to the desert mountains, and snaked north all the way to Tel Aviv. Early in the afternoon another soldier gave Aron a lift in a jeep to the main road. From there Aron knew he would have to hitchhike his way home. Normally, in Israel, civilians will readily pick up a soldier on leave, so he didn't expect that to be any problem.

Aron stood alone at the edge of the road. Even though he was quite visibly in uniform, surprisingly trucks and cars passed him by. No one, it seemed, would stop to give him a ride. Some of the trucks did slow down, but as they came closer invariably they would pick up speed. He couldn't understand it.

It started to get dark, and with the coming of night Aron started to worry. This area was known to be very dangerous. Unpredictable Arab attacks from across the border were all too frequent.

The next time Aron saw a truck coming toward him,

he raised his Uzi automatic weapon and aimed it directly at the vehicle's tires, motioning that if the driver failed to stop he was going to shoot out the tires.

The truck came to a screeching halt.

Aron jumped up into the truck's cab. He looked at the driver. "I'm going to Kastina," he said. It was a camp some twenty kilometers up the road. "If you let me out there, it will be fine."

The driver nodded, and the truck rolled forward.

As they drove, Aron said angrily, "What kind of people are you? I was trying to get a lift for hours. No one would stop for me. You know how dangerous this place can be. If I hadn't threatened you, you wouldn't have stopped for me, either."

"Listen, soldier," growled the truck driver. "Plenty of Arabs are doing the same thing."

"What do you mean?"

The driver looked at him with surprise. "Don't you know? It's common practice for an infiltrator to kill one of our soldiers, dress in his uniform, then, as an Israeli soldier, they stand by the road, and wait to hijack a truck."

Very late that night Aron reached his home. His wife threw her arms around him, and his baby smiled gleefully.

Aron worked on the farm all of Saturday and Sunday, completing the necessary chores. By Monday morning, as promised, he was back at the army base.

Aron received leave once again. It was a Friday night, and Ester was anxiously waiting for Aron to return. Hours passed but he didn't arrive. Ester was frightened.

She decided to contact the local army headquarters for information. The sergeant on duty informed her that Aron had indeed been granted a week's leave.

Now Ester was frantic. The army presumed Aron to

be lost, and feared dead. They searched for him for an entire week. It was not uncommon for soldiers to be murdered by Arabs hiding in the hills.

Ten days elapsed. Aron walked in his front door. He was greeted by stares of shock and joy.

Ester's mouth was wide open. Her eyes grew luminous in relief. Her prayers had been answered.

Aron had no idea of what was happening. Apparently, there had been a bureaucratic mix-up somewhere along the way. Aron's commander had ordered his squad away for ten days of special and secret maneuvers. He, apparently, had *not* been granted home leave. No one, though, had known anything about this.

A soldier's life in the Israeli Army is always perilous. Aron's specialty was sweeping fields for hidden mines, and also the placing of their own. On one particular occasion his squad was sent out at night on maneuvers to a location somewhere within territory Israel had briefly occupied and with which they were not familiar. They were dropped off, and then instructed to find their own way back to the base camp. The journey home took several long, hazardous days. They were in constant danger of being spotted by Jordanian Army patrols guarding the frontier.

At one other time his company had been ordered to join a convoy from their base, moving south to a location in the harsh Negev desert. A sergeant whom Aron knew, told him that along the way they would be passing the vicinity of his village. In fact, they would, at one point, be no more than a kilometer from his own farm.

Aron laughingly suggested that the convoy stop to have their lunch at his farm. To his surprise and delight the officers in command agreed.

Two hundred men, all well armed, in jeeps and anti-tank vehicles, entered the village and on to Aron's farm. Neither Ester, or their neighbors could imagine what was happening. Was an Arab attack on their village imminent? Had the country been forced to go to war again?

No, Aron gleefully informed them. They had merely stopped by for lunch.

The company of soldiers spent an hour and a half relaxing and eating, before they were off again. The sudden appearance of the convoy at their home was one of the biggest thrills Aron and Ester had ever shared.

Time passed. Israel was growing rapidly, new towns, new industries, sprouting like grass. And Aron was extremely proud that he had now become a small but integral part of this great land. He longed for nothing more than to see young Morris grow up together with his country. He could visualize both his son and himself, living their entire lives as free men, in this new nation. He would gladly spend the rest of his days here, were it not for his brother, Abe.

Aron had been in Israel for only a short time when Abe left for America. Soon after his departure his brother was writing letters regularly to Aron pleading with him to join him in New York.

It was not an easy decision for Aron to make. Nor would it ever be. The bonds between the two brothers were as strong as ever, despite the distance that separated them. For five years Aron had remained in Israel, wishing to stay among his fellow Jews in the newly created Jewish state.

Abe persistently pleaded. "I need you here with me," he would write. "Our family should be together."

Aron refused to change his mind. It wasn't practical; not with a family. He had responsibilities. There were others to consider now, not only himself.

There were many more imploring letters. "If anything should happen to you while serving in the Israeli army, I would never forgive myself," Abe would say. "Not now. Not after all the suffering we shared. . . ."

On one sunny, warm day Aron sat on the front steps of his small house, exhausted from worrying about the problems that were currently confronting him and his small family. He looked rather surprised as his mailman strolled up to him and delivered yet another letter.

"This is for you, Aron," he said with a smile, handing him the envelope.

He took the letter, held it in his hand and stared down at the overseas postmark.

The stamps were American. Aron opened his mail, and as he slowly read the letter he could feel Abe's sorrow and genuine concern in the words he wrote.

Aron found himself crying as he read.

"You won't have to worry about anything," the letter stated. "I have enough money to pay all your expenses to come to New York. I want so much for us to be reunited, Aron. *Please*, my brother, come here so we can be together again. . . ."

Aron knew that he had come so far and waited so long to reach his present status. Was it worth it, he wondered. Was it worth one more gamble. To leave everything and everyone behind, uproot the family and resettle in America?

After much consideration and soul searching, he decided to take the chance, after all. To be reunited with Abe again, and begin new lives for himself and his family.

After supper he and Ester sat outside. A blazing Middle Eastern sun was setting in a magnificent magenta sky. Evening stars were already appearing. They sat quietly for a time. Ester saw that Aron seemed troubled.

"Are you worrying again?"

He made a small gesture with his hand, indicating that he wasn't.

"I know you, Aron. Something is bothering you. Tell me what's the matter."

He inhaled deeply as he gazed out at the rows of newly planted trees. He felt unsure of how he should break the news, and even more uncertain about her reaction. "You're right, Ester. We do have to talk."

She smiled, "so talk."

"I. . . . I'm thinking of leaving."

"The farm?" She squeezed his arm. "It'll work out. It's just going to take longer than we thought. We'll make it work. You'll see."

"No, it isn't the farm."

Her smile vanished. Was something seriously wrong? Had something happened about which she knew nothing?

"I received another letter today," he said, reassuring her. "Abe wants me to be with him."

"Abe's always asking you to do that." A letter from Aron's brother was no surprise by any means, and she was relieved to hear that it was nothing more.

He looked into her eyes, making her face him squarely. "This time it was different. There was something in his words, something I can't fully express to you. Ester, this isn't easy for me, for any of us. But I believe it's the right thing to do. I've been thinking about it all day. It's all I've thought about. I love you, and want to do what's best for our family, you know that, don't you?"

"Of course I know that."

"Then you'll understand." He took a deep breath. This wasn't going to be easy for him at all.

"I'll understand everything better if you tell me what you're trying to say. . . ."

"I'm going to tell Abe that I'll come. As soon as I can complete all the necessary arrangements, and make sure that you and Morris are properly looked after while I'm away."

"America?" said Ester. "You've decided to go after all?"

Aron nodded. "America. New York."

They had heard so many wonderful things about this exciting, bold nation. It offered so much promise to all of its citizens. The economic leader of the free world. The richest nation on the face of the earth. The arguments in favor of going were forceful and compelling.

"Are you sure about this, Aron?" There was a hint of tears in her eyes. "Is it really what you want?"

"I didn't say it would be easy for you. Or for any of us."

"And what about my parents and family? Do you expect me to pick up and leave them behind, just like that?"

He held her tenderly, stroking her hair. "Perhaps, with luck, we'll bring them to America in time. Maybe even in a year or two. If there *is* any way to do it, I promise that I'll find it."

"What will you do there, Aron? What sort of work? You don't even speak the language."

He sat thoughtfully before answering her. "I'll do whatever God wills. Whatever it takes. But I do believe we should give it a try, as Abe asks me. Perhaps America will be our destiny after all. . . ."

Ester realized that her husband was determined. She still wasn't quite certain that it was the right thing to do, yet she knew Aron well enough to know that he means whatever he says.

"All right, Aron. If you honestly think it's best. I'll not try to stop you."

Soon after, Ester, and Morris, now four years old, tearfully waved goodbye to him at Israel's Lod airport. They watched the airplane rise into the clouds, and slowly disappear.

It was a Thursday. The date was February 20. The year was 1956. Aron arrived in the United States. Both his brothers were waiting to greet him.

As he was ready to disembark, he fondly recalled Papa's words:

Go, my son. Maybe you will survive. . . .

Aron smiled and forgot his fears.

His long journey was over at last.

Chapter Twenty Two

NEW YORK CITY, 1978

Aron sat at his kitchen table drinking coffee. Warm morning sunlight filtered through the windows of his Bayside, Queens, home. It was going to be a nice day.

The telephone rang. "It's for you," said Ester. "It's Abe."

Aron pushed his newspaper aside, and took the phone. Abe had recently retired, and was looking forward to a full, active life during his golden years. "How are you, Abe?"

"How are *you* doing?"

The tone of his voice jolted Aron. He knew his older brother better than anyone, and he could tell that something was wrong. "Abe, what's happened? Are you ill? Should I come over—"

"No, Aron. I'm all right. Really. Just that last night I

had this dream Aron . . ." There was a great deal of emotion in his quivering voice, and Aron knew that his brother was fighting back tears. "I dreamed about Itzhak. He came to me, standing right before me. Tearfully, Itzhak said to me, 'How much longer are you going to leave me here?' . . ."

Aron felt chills. "Abe, Abe listen to me. I want you to come over to my office today. We have to talk."

"Aron, the dream was so real. Itzhak was so real."

"I know, Abe. That's why I'm asking you to meet me. Today; this morning. Will you come?"

"I'll be there," said Abe.

Aron hung up. Ester was staring at him. He tried to avoid her gaze. Suddenly, his mind was reeling, and he recalled an incident that had happened twenty-two years ago, in 1956, the same year that he arrived in the United States.

Aron had been working in his brother's small shop in New York's garment center. He was a leather cutter, using the patterns for the leather jackets that his brother manufactured, working long hours to support his newly arrived family.

On that particular day he and his brother were going to lunch in a local busy cafeteria on Eighth Avenue. As they entered, another customer was hastily leaving. The man on his way out caught sight of their faces and froze in his steps. "My God," he cried. "Aren't you Aron Goldfarb? Aren't you Abe?"

Aron stared. His eyes narrowed. "Jack Baum," he whispered.

Jack Baum nodded. "Yes, it's me."

This man, Jack Baum, had worked in the blacksmith shop in Pionki, with Itzhak. They had been good friends. It was an incredible coincidence; after some thirty-four years, thousands of miles away from their birthplaces, they met on a street in New York. It was a moment for tears and joy. After so long, so much.

It was unbelievable.

They stood outside on the street corner talking, oblivious to the bustling world around them.

"Abe, Aron," cried Jack Baum, "It's a miracle to find you here alive, both of you."

"And you, Jack," exclaimed Abe with equal ardor. "I can't believe it."

He smiled at the sight of his old friends. They had changed a great deal, he knew, and so had he. He would never forget them. "Please, Jack, tell me how you managed to survive."

"Abe, Abe," he said in a choked voice. "I have so much to tell you. So much." Jack drew a deep breath, unsure of where to start. "All right. I'll tell you everything."

"After you, your brothers, and friends escaped, everyone in Pionki was happy for you. Some were envious. But everyone blessed you, predicting that you would all be the only Jews to survive the war.

"As it turned out, though, most of the Pionki Jews managed to survive. The Nazis were sending Pionki's Jews to Auschwitz, to the gas chambers. However, at the time of your escape, the Germans were on the run from the Allies. So most were spared."

An incredible irony, Abe knew. Had the three brothers remained inside the labor camp, Itzhak might very likely still be alive.

"Is that what happened to you? You were shipped to a death camp?"

Jack Baum shook his head. "Only a few days after you fled, I also did the same. I ran for refuge into the forest. I was without food and proper clothing. There was no way I was going to survive. I collapsed, certain

234

that I would be dead by morning. A Christian farmer chanced by and found me lying there. He put me into his wagon, and took me to his home. He hid me in his attic with several other Jews. This farmer, this wonderful Christian named Jan Sot, saved my life. He rescued other Jews as well. I shall never forget him. I write to him, even now, and I pray for him.

"Jan Sot had a daughter. She was an angel, this girl. She would bring us food, sing to us, and try and buoy our spirits. There were some good Polish Christians, Abe. Jan Sot, though, was the finest I ever knew. The AK were suspicious of him. But they could never prove that he was harboring Jews, so they used to beat him badly." Jack Baum's lips quivered as he spoke, and more tears ran down his face. "Jan never gave any of us away. No matter what the AK said, or what they threatened and did to him . . ."

"He must be a very special man, Jack."

"He is. Very much so to everyone who knew him." He collected his thoughts, so grateful to have had so many blessings. All the more now, with the meeting of these very old friends. "And Itzhak, where is my friend Itzhak?" he asked excitedly.

Abe lowered his eyes. He put his hand on Jack Baum's shoulder. "I'm sorry, my dear friend. I didn't realize. But of course, you didn't know. You would have no way of knowing. Itzhak is dead. He and our friend Zisman Berman were killed in 1944, after we escaped from Pionki. It was in August. At the village of Kfatki. Murdered by AK partisans."

Jack Baum paled. He began to shake. He put his hands to his face and sobbed bitterly. In those terrible times at Pionki he and Itzhak Goldfarb had become close comrades, sharing much of each other's lives. "Abe, listen to me," he cried out in anguish. "I was in

235

Kfatki. That's where I was hiding, and I saw it. Do you understand me? I saw your brother being killed—only I didn't know it was him." He sobbed again.

Abe went into shock, unable to talk.

"It's God's, truth, Abe. I was looking through the slats of the attic window on that very day. Below, in the street, I saw two young men running. They headed for the field. I saw them gunned down." He trembled and continued to weep. "I had no idea it was Itzhak. No idea at all. I ran and told Jan Sot about the killings. Later, the farmer went out with his young son, Wacek. They took their wagon, picked up the bodies and buried them nearby. . . ."

Aron distanced himself from his memories. Itzhak had been dead for almost thirty-five years. That chance encounter with Jack Baum had taken place more than twenty years ago. None of the brothers kept in touch with Jack. Now, however, these events were coming back to haunt him, and he knew that their lives would intertwine again.

Aron sat at his desk looking at his distraught brother. Abe was disheveled and quite upset, Aron could hardly recognize him. His mind was not peaceful, but then, neither was Aron's. None of their family had received a proper burial. They knew that the ashes of Papa, their sisters, and youngest brother, were somewhere near Treblinka. There was no possibility of burying them. With Itzhak, though, it was different. He and Zisman were buried by the kindly farmer, Jan Sot. His remains, and Zisman's, would still be there in the cold earth of Poland.

Aron was remorseful. Why hadn't they buried Itzhak and Zisman properly?

Poland remained a place of horrible memories, one

that none of the brothers wanted to see again. Yet, some unfinished business remained, Aron knew that neither he, Abe, nor brother Jacob could rest until they did what must be done.

"Abe," said Aron at length, "Let's get Jacob on the phone. We've got plans to make. We're returning to Poland."

Aron could not find the location mentioned by Jack Baum, the only man who could provide the answers they needed. He phoned the Yiddish language newspaper in New York, the *Jewish Daily Forward*, and asked if there was a society of survivors from the town of Kelc, where Jack Baum had lived. There was such an organization, and the newspaper was happy to provide them with the telephone number of its president.

"Of course I know Jack Baum," the president told Aron on the phone. "He lives in Queens, but listen, Jack has not been well. In fact, he's quite ill."

"I understand," replied Aron. And with this new information he called Jack Baum.

"This is Aron Goldfarb, Jack. Do you remember me?"

The voice at the other end was tremulous and hesitant. "Aron? No, I don't think I know who you are . . ."

"Then do you remember my brother Itzhak? You worked with him in the blacksmith shop in Pionki. Itzhak Goldfarb."

At the mention of the name, Jack Baum burst into tears. "Oh my God, of course. Of course I remember Itzhak."

"Listen to me, Jack. I need to speak with you. It's very important. Can we meet somewhere? I'll come to your home, if you like."

"I've been very sick, you know, but if you want, give

me your address. I'm still working in the city," then he added, "If you're planning to go to Poland, don't expect any help from me."

Aron was surprised, "but why not?, we just want to find Itzhak's remains . . ."

"I will not do anything for you. Returning to Poland is death for all of our Jews. Even now. You know how they hate us . . ." Jack Baum was genuinely concerned for their safety.

"Jack, I promise you, we'll have protection. Police, American Embassy people, whatever is necessary. No harm will come to us, but please, Jack, there are some things I must know, and you're the only one who can tell me."

Soon after this conversation, Aron and his brothers met with the ailing man. He repeated for them, in detail, all of the facts regarding Itzhak and Zisman's deaths. He wept as he spoke. Without being aware of it, Aron found himself crying as well.

"Here is Jan Sot's address," Jack Baum said at last. "I still write to the family, even send them money. I don't know if Jan is still alive or not."

"We'll find out for you."

"Then remember to mention me. I used a false name during those months; a Polish name. Janek, they knew me as. Janek Kowalski."

Aron nodded his understanding. "All right. I'll send them a letter of my own, and tell his family that we are friends of their friend, Janek Kowalski. Thank you, Jack, for everything. You've greatly lightened our burden."

A letter was sent to New York's Senator Jacob Javits, explaining the situation. If it was going to be necessary for them to deal with the Polish Communist authori-

238

ties, they knew they'd need as much help as they could get. Abe requested assistance from the State Department. In addition they all visited the Polish Consulate in New York.

"Why did you wait so long?" a consular official asked in a friendly manner.

After that, it was on to the Polish Embassy in Washington D.C. The Assistant Secretary for Foreign Affairs promised that he would do everything possible to help in the matter. Even with all this cooperation, long months elapsed. Senator Javits' intercession proved invaluable. He helped open many doors to cut through the mass of red tape. Aron was very grateful.

He wrote to Jan Sot's family, and soon received a reply.

"My husband is dead," the widow informed them. But if you come, my family and I will do all we can to help." The letter touched Aron deeply. At times he would forget that there were still good, kind people in the world.

It took several weeks for the State Department to prepare all the necessary documents.

It was in the early summer of 1978, that Aron, Abe, and Jacob arrived in the land of their birth. They unpacked their bags at the Hotel Forum, a simple, unadorned and cold place. They informed the American Consul of their itinerary and the purpose of their mission. The Embassy asked them to contact them again immediately upon their return.

A taxi driven by a pleasant fellow named Tadek was hired. They left the city very early the morning, and drove south, towards Kfatki. Along the way they passed Pionki. All traces of the former labor camp were gone. Great factories were now part of the landscape. There was, however, no monument of remembrance.

It was as if Nazi Pionki had never existed. Turned into ashes and scattered by the winds, like crematorium remains of the Jewish people. Aron paled as they passed that dreaded place. He never imagined that he would ever return.

Memories flooded his mind and overwhelmed him. He remembered places, faces and names he had long buried away.

At length the taxi reached the village of Pionki. They asked a local farmer where the Sot family lived.

"Right over there," he pointed.

With baited breath Aron knocked on the door. A frail, elderly woman greeted them.

"Good morning, madam. We're Janek Kowalski's friends. I wrote to you . . ."

"Please, come in."

They stepped inside the little house. The Sot's were poor simple people. Good people. Aron gave her the presents and money they had brought for her and her family.

"Janek told me that he survived only because you and your husband were so kind and caring.

Tearfully she said in a shaky voice, "the AK used to come here, they would beat my husband viciously, and accuse him of hiding Jews, and of being a traitor. Never did Jan betray anyone. Never."

A lump rose in Aron's throat. "I know that, Mrs. Sot. I know that." He sighed. "We're here to find the remains of our brother. We know your husband and son buried them somewhere in the nearby woods."

Even before Aron could finish, Jan Sot's son, Wacek, came through the door.

She fed them with sour milk and bread while they spoke with Jan's son.

"I can find the place we buried your brother with

my eyes closed," Wacek told them. The memory of that event was vivid in his mind. "It's very close by. Perhaps one kilometer from here. I'll take you there now, if you like."

The moment they had waited for, anticipated for so long, had finally arrived. Aron rose, his knees trembling. "We're going to need some shovels."

"I have shovels," replied Wacek. "There should be no problem in finding your brother's remains."

Abe began to sob unashamedly. The emotion of this long awaited moment left him helpless.

Aron and Jacob went outside. Abe walked shakily behind them. Accompanied by Tadek and Jan's son, they began their walk across the fields. As they finally approached the treeline of the woods, Wacek stopped and pointed to a clump of trees. "There, between those trees, that's where they're buried."

Abe was transfixed. Aron, Jacob and the others took shovels, slowly made their way to the indicated place, and started to dig.

It did not take long for them to dig a hole about one meter deep. Nothing was found. Suddenly, Aron's shovel hit something. He carefully removed soil from around the object; a skull appeared. Then a second one was found. Soon a number of scattered bones were unearthed.

The brothers stared down. They cried bitterly at the pitiful discovery, reliving the nightmare of those terrible years. The unbearable times they all shared and had so long buried but never quite forgot.

We've come for you, Itzhak, Aron said to himself. *Soon you'll be able to rest in peace. We're together at last.*

"Get blankets," cried Jacob suddenly. "Something in which to carry away the remains right now! We'll take them to Warsaw and then on to New York."

"No," said Aron. "They won't allow us do that. We'll have to report it openly to the Polish authorities, and to their Department of Health. I know it won't be easy for us. We'll have to go through official channels and probably some red tape, but there's no other way."

He was right, Jacob knew. There was no alternative. It had been their intention to have Itzhak and Zisman buried in the proper Jewish tradition, safely, in the land of Israel. To take any chances now might jeopardize everything.

They covered over the grave site with earth, and marked it. Aron prayed for the strength to do what had to be done.

They returned to Warsaw, and went to the Department of Health's Special Section for Survivors, which helped to locate family graves of the war. The official on duty greeted them politely. He had only one arm, and Aron wondered how he'd lost the other one. Perhaps he, too, had suffered at the hands of the Nazis.

"We are here to appeal for your assistance," Aron told the man. "We have found the grave of our brother and friend. They were murdered in 1944 by members of the AK."

The government man became visibly upset. "The AK was not an organization of killers," he informed them tersely. "They were Poland's partisans. Our freedom fighters. They strove to rid our land of fascists."

"Indeed?" said Aron. He recalled his own experiences only too well. However this was neither the time nor place to argue the matter. "We wish to have their remains sent to the State of Israel for burial."

"This is very difficult, and very expensive," the man said. "One of you will have to take another officer back to the grave to certify it. As you probably know, Po-

242

land has no diplomatic relations with Israel. The Embassy of Holland is serving as the intermediary for Israel's matters."

The red tape had started.

The Dutch were as helpful as possible. "We need to arrange all this with the Government of Israel. It should take from four to six months, if all goes well. You understand how it is with these things?"

"Yes," said Aron. "We understand."

"Go home, and as soon as everything is in order, we'll notify you."

Aron, Abe and Jacob remained in Poland for ten days, visiting old friends like Jan Koptera, and the site of Treblinka where Papa and the others were killed. They wept beside the monument for the dead of their home town of Bialobrzegi. It was a painful experience but a catharsis for all of them.

It was some five months later, back in New York, when the official letter for which they had all been waiting, arrived. Abe and Jacob left for Israel to make the arrangements. They purchased a cemetery plot in the scenic town of Holon. There was more red tape to overcome, but the remains finally arrived in a sealed aluminum box.

A large notice was placed in *Davar,* one of Tel Aviv's leading newspapers. It mentioned the place, date and time of the burial of Itzhak Goldfarb and their good friend Zisman Berman.

Aron arrived in Israel to join his waiting brothers.

The funeral service was scheduled for three in the afternoon. Many people attended, some from distant places in Israel. There would be only one grave for the two young men, as it had been impossible to establish their identities. They would be buried together, as brothers. An Orthodox rabbi conducted the prayers.

243

As Aron stood weeping among the crowd, he suddenly heard his name being called.

"Goldfarb! Where is Goldfarb?"

Abe stepped forward. "I'm Abe Goldfarb," he said.

A small teary-eyed woman perhaps in her mid-forties walked to the front and approached the brothers. "I'm Zisman's sister," she announced. She was a very religious woman, Aron noticed, and standing beside her was a tall young man wearing an Israeli army uniform. His rank was captain. Aron could see that the woman was very proud of her son, and as he thought of Zisman, he knew that his good friend would also join her.

"God bless you for bringing our brother home," she wept.

It was a long, and extremely sad, day. In the crowd were other survivors from Pionki, good friends of Aron's, Chaim Goldberg, and Meyer Cohen.

They stood together in silence as the prayers were recited. All of them, reunited after thirty-five years. Aron, through his tears and pain, felt renewed. His work was completed at last.

His brother and friend were at finally at rest in their own country. And he knew that as long as there is a Jewish people, as long as there is an Israel, Itzhak and Zisman will live forever in loving memory.

Afterword

In 1956, Aron Goldfarb arrived in the United States to join his brother and lifelong friend, Abe. He found a job immediately. Within seven months he was able to send for Ester, and his son, Morris.

Eager to work for himself, Aron found a partner, and in 1958 went into the business of manufacturing leather jackets in the garment center of New York. He struggled for many years to keep the business solvent, and to see it grow. Good breaks were few and far between. Aron, however, was persistent. His small company was called G&N.

Soon after his arrival in the United States, Aron and Ester had a second son. He was born on August 10, 1957. They named him Ira, after Itzhak.

Some sixteen years later, Morris began to work for his father. A bright youth with his father's zeal, he

245

quickly became a valuable asset, for what was now known as G-III Leather Fashions.

In 1989 G-III, now one of the most successful manufacturers of quality leather coats and jackets in the United States, became a public corporation. It is now known as the G-III Apparel Group, Ltd., and employs more than three hundred people in New York. G-III's overseas operations employ several thousands more in Korea. It is a business that currently grosses some two hundred million dollars a year.

Aron often thinks back to those painful years of the war, and the tragic losses not only in his own family, but also of so many millions of others, Jews and Christians alike, whose lives were so needlessly ended. He wonders if those people had survived, how many would have increased or added to the collective knowledge and culture of mankind. How many scientists among them who might have found cures for diseases. How many doctors who might have eased the afflictions of others who live with pain. Educators, who could have taught the disadvantaged. Clergymen who would have provided hope and faith to their communities. Businessmen, like himself, who provide work for so many who might otherwise have remained in poverty, but now live good and decent lives. Writers, artists, musicians, creators of all kinds, who could have added so much culture to the world. Men and women of law, architects, and builders whose contributions will never be seen. He understands that it is humanity itself which has suffered the most by the loss of so many of their brothers and sisters.

Aron currently lives a quiet, simple life. With good reason, he is quite proud of his achievements, and those of his sons. He and Ester have five grandchildren whom they love dearly. The legacy of his father remains stronger than ever. And with that memory, he knows that all his family survive within him.

Aron resides in New York City, but makes frequent trips back to Israel, where his beloved brother, Itzhak, and their friend, Zisman, are in peace.